PROFESSION: JOURNALIST

PROFESSION: JOURNALIST

A study on the working conditions of journalists

G. Bohère

International Labour Office   Geneva

Copyright © International Labour Organisation 1984

Publications of the International Labour Office enjoy copyright under Protocol 2 of the Universal Copyright Convention. Nevertheless, short excerpts from them may be reproduced without authorisation, on condition that the source is indicated. For rights of reproduction or translation, application should be made to the Publications Branch (Rights and Permissions), International Labour Office, CH-1211 Geneva 22, Switzerland. The International Labour Office welcomes such applications.

ISBN 92-2-103531-X

First published 1984

Originally published in French under the title:
Profession: Journaliste (ISBN 92-2-203531-3)

The designations employed in ILO publications, which are in conformity with United Nations practice, and the presentation of material therein do not imply the expression of any opinion whatsoever on the part of the International Labour Office concerning the legal status of any country or territory or of its authorities, or concerning the delimitation of its frontiers.
The responsibility for opinions expressed in signed articles, studies and other contributions rests solely with their authors, and publication does not constitute an endorsement by the International Labour Office of the opinions expressed in them.

ILO publications can be obtained through major booksellers or ILO local offices in many countries, or direct from ILO Publications, International Labour Office, CH-1211 Geneva 22, Switzerland. A catalogue or list of new publications will be sent free of charge from the above address.

Printed in Switzerland

FOREWORD

The present study is the fifth which the ILO has devoted to journalists. The four previous ones cover only a limited number of years and already date back half a century. The first study, which was published in 1928 and widely distributed, dealt with working and living conditions.[1] The second, which was submitted in 1928 to what was then the Advisory Committee on Professional Workers, was a brief report on the "conscience clause" and was completed the following year by an additional note. A third report, dealing with the unemployment of professional workers, produced in 1929 for the same Committee, contained a monograph on unemployed journalists. Finally, in 1931, a report on journalists' collective contracts was submitted to the Committee.

Subsequently, the Advisory Committee on Salaried Employees and Professional Workers, which, after the Second World War, replaced the two committees that had previously dealt with employees and professional workers, requested a special meeting to examine problems concerning the profession of journalism. The ILO has not yet been able to convene such a meeting.

Once again, 50 years later, the ILO is returning to the question of the situation of the journalist as a worker. Such is the scope and complexity of the subject that it has not been possible to cover it completely. For example, the question of author's rights for journalists has been omitted. Nor has it been possible to give adequate attention to the specific problems of the employment of journalists in the audio-visual media.

The author has based his study on general documentation drawn from books, magazines and various reports, on conversations with members of the profession, on an analysis of laws and collective agreements and, finally, on information obtained in reply to a questionnaire distributed for the most part through the ILO field offices in 1978; all this information has since been updated to the fullest extent possible.

Profession: Journalist

Sincere thanks are due to governmental services, professional organisations and individuals who have contributed to this volume of information.

Note

[1] ILO: *Conditions of work and life of journalists,* Studies and Reports, Series L (Professional Workers), No. 2 (Geneva, 1928).

CONTENTS

Foreword v

Introduction 1

1. **Structure of the profession** 7
   Range of definitions in the profession 7
      Professional status 10
      Types of employer 12
   Variety of functions 14
      Editor 14
      Sub-editor 15
      Reporter 16
      Radio and television journalist 17
   Range of training 17
      Initial training 17
      Training within the profession 23
   Working for more than one employer 27

2. **Employment in the profession** 33
   Society and the press 33
   Number of journalists 40

3. **Technological and economic constraints and employment problems** . . 45
   Technological evolution 45
   Economic constraints 55
   Extent of unemployment among journalists 59

4. **Ethical standards in the profession** 63
   Codes of ethics 63
   The conscience clause 68

5. The career and its problems — 71
- Recruitment — 72
- Advancement and mobility in the profession — 74
  - Promotion — 74
  - Moving up the ladder, service bonuses — 75
  - Grades — 76
  - Professional mobility — 77
- Advanced training — 78
- Equality of opportunity between men and women — 83

6. Weekly hours of work, time off per week and annual paid leave — 85
- Weekly hours of work — 85
- Time off per week — 87
- Annual paid leave — 92

7. Pay — 99
- Basic salary — 100
- Compensation for overtime — 103
- Bonuses and allowances — 107
  - Cost of living allowance — 107
  - Additional pay for long service — 108
  - Participation in profits and performance or merit bonuses — 108
  - Allowances for professional expenses — 110
- Payment of freelance journalists — 111
- Women's salaries — 112

8. Safety and health — 115
- Safety — 115
- Health and well-being — 118

9. Termination of employment — 123
- Resignation — 123
- Dismissal — 126
  - Grounds for dismissal — 126
  - Notice — 128
  - Severance pay — 130

10. Social security — 133

11. Industrial relations — 141
- Trade unionism among journalists — 141
  - International organisations — 146
- Some aspects of collective bargaining — 147
  - Scope of application — 148
  - Procedures — 149

Content 150
Freelance journalists and collective bargaining 151
Labour disputes 152
Participation of journalists in decision-making 157

Conclusion 169

Appendix — Extracts from the *Compendium of principles and good practices relating to the conditions of work and employment of professional workers*, adopted by an ILO Tripartite Meeting on Conditions of Work and Employment of Professional Workers (Geneva, 22-30 November 1977) 173

Tables

1. Distribution of journalists among the information media in selected countries (in actual numbers or percentages) 13
2. United Kingdom: Educational level of reporters under training, 1964-75 (in percentages) 19
3. Number and circulation of daily newspapers and other periodicals by country 34
4. Number and circulation of daily newspapers by regions, groups and countries 39
5. Numbers of journalists in selected countries 42
6. Normal hours of work and time off per week 90
7. Annual paid leave 93
8. Compensation for overtime, night work, Sunday work and work on public holidays 104
9. Period of notice (resignation and dismissal) 124
10. Severance pay in case of dismissal or redundancy 130

INTRODUCTION

Literate people in ancient Rome could learn the latest news by reading wall posters. In comparison with mere oral transmission, some progress had already been made. However, oral transmission remained the principal means of communication and the age of rapid, mass dissemination of information was still far off. That point was not reached until the appearance of typography in the fifteenth century, the establishment of postal services by certain European States at about the same time and the inquisitive minds and agile pens of several generations of "newshounds", "gazetteers" and "sleuths" in the following centuries. The recognition of freedom of expression was equally important, even if it was frequently eclipsed. And finally, and perhaps particularly, the reading habit had to be sufficiently developed to justify large circulations, which themselves could only become a reality with the invention in the nineteenth century of the rotary printing machine and linotype. There were also purely economic and commercial factors, such as the reduction in the selling price of newspapers in relation to the purchasing power of potential readers, or the development of distribution networks — by rail, road and air.

As these conditions gradually came about, the press extended its influence and asserted its role in society as a medium of information and opinion, thus earning for itself the title of the Fourth Estate.

The importance of the printed or spoken press in modern life cannot be measured simply by numbers of copies or circulation figures, or by the density of radios or television sets. The nature of its functions must also be taken into account: the press informs, influences public opinion, instructs and entertains.

The press informs. On this particular point, no effort will be made to determine to what extent radio (or television), which can capture the event and transmit it instantaneously, has supplanted the newspaper; equally, no attempt will be made to define in which areas of information the press is irreplaceable. Looked at overall, the primary role of the

Profession: Journalist

printed or spoken press is to announce what has happened, and what possible events are to be expected, on the international, national or local level, and in all sectors: political, economic, social, artistic, religious, sporting, scientific, etc. It also provides practical information. In this context, the local press plays an indispensable service role in announcing cinema programmes, the names of pharmacies open after normal hours, regional weather forecasts, times of high and low tides, etc. Thus, the temporary absence of newspapers is keenly felt — in times of strike for example.

The press helps in forming opinion. Not only does it inform, but it also explains and comments, and the distinction between information and comment is not easy to make. By its selection and presentation of news, the press exercises a strong influence on public opinion and, as a side-effect, on the development of events. There are innumerable personalities in the business world, in arts or in politics who owe their success or disappointments to information or comments carried by newspapers.

The press instructs and entertains. The great numbers of reports in major daily and weekly newspapers of a general information nature, together with those in numerous specialised periodicals, provide readers with a veritable encyclopaedia, continuously renewed and updated, in which they can find both information and entertainment. There is little doubt that such newspapers represent one of the most rewarding sources of what might be called "parallel education".

The press is thus an extremely effective instrument of communication and it is not hard to understand why sociologists — to mention purely disinterested observers — are so keen to describe and analyse the influence of newspapers. The object of the present study is not to probe deeper into that area but to examine one of the driving forces of this influence. Like all enterprises, a newspaper is a combination of two elements: capital and human resources. This study will focus on the second element and, among the various categories in that context, on the journalist only. Administrative and printing staff are not referred to here since their problems are of a different nature, although it should not be overlooked that events affecting the economic life of a newspaper and those affecting other categories of staff, printers in particular, can have repercussions on the situation of journalists. Moreover, while journalists as a whole are taken into consideration, the study is primarily concerned with those who handle current news on a daily basis, such as news agency and daily newspaper journalists in the printed or audio-visual media.

Information of this kind is a perishable product. It is produced for immediate consumption. If it fails to reach the market in good time, the consumers lose interest, since their attention is diverted to fresher news. If news is not exploited immediately, it is "spiked", unless it is

Introduction

of prime importance, and even then it rapidly ceases to be "hot" news and, if it is not consigned to history, comes under another aspect of journalism.

For the same reason, news is a product in fierce competition. It has to be delivered at least as fast as the products of other manufacturers and, if possible, before.

This speed of execution is one of the features of the life of a daily newspaper and, as a result, dominates the work pace of the life of a journalist.

It is a demanding and sometimes dangerous profession and yet attracts more applicants than it can absorb. This is no doubt due to such factors as the responsibility of the job, a certain authority it gives, contact with events and with those who bring them about, the apparent variety of activity (for even journalism can be monotonous on occasions) and the sense of adventure.

And yet this profession has its humble workers who, in fact, are in the great majority. Alongside a few editorial star writers, columnists and big-name foreign newspaper or television correspondents are the obscure masses of agency writers, sub-editors, general reporters, etc., whose joint effort tends to shape and standardise production. These are the people who go from one employer to another, rather like the office furniture and the rotary machines, at the mercy of take-overs and regroupings — if indeed such operations do not leave them without a job.

An intellectual and even creative profession, journalism would at first sight seem badly adapted to the labyrinth of regulations which determine working conditions in most other sectors of activity. At first it did avoid most of them, at least to a large extent, but it is now coming increasingly under their control. The need to adjust working hours to getting the newspaper out on the streets; the fact that most journalists are salaried workers and that their interests do not always coincide with those of their employers; the modern tendency to regulate working life down to the last detail; the interdependence of professional categories; the growing complexity of society: all these factors, and others, encourage the development of a tight network of specific legislative and contractual arrangements, not to mention regulations of a general nature which apply as much to the journalist as to any other salaried worker.

Apart from certain problems which find their solution in other juridical spheres — author's rights, for example, which fall under the heading of intellectual property — most of the employment and working conditions of journalists are dealt with under the general legislation for workers. Additional arrangements, which vary in degree of detail, are provided by specific laws on the press, by collective agreements and individual contracts, or by one or the other.

Among the special laws for press workers, the following can be quoted:

- the Argentine law of 1946 *(Estatuto del Periodista Profesional)* which deals with the main aspects of employment and working conditions;
- the section for professional journalists in the French Labour Code on the cancellation of contracts, remuneration, leave and professional identity cards;
- the Indian Working Journalists (Conditions of Service) and Miscellaneous Provisions Act of 1955 for journalists and other newspaper employees which fixes conditions for the termination of employment, maximum working hours and the right to paid leave, and which envisages the establishment of a Wage Board; [1]
- the decree of 1974 setting up a charter for the press in Madagascar which, in addition to the duties and obligations mentioned above, defines the rights of journalists with regard to dismissal, taxation, insurance against unusual risks, and author's rights;
- the Pakistan law of 1973 on press employees which sets up a salaries committee responsible for fixing salary levels for newspaper staff, journalists and other employees, and which regulates other aspects of conditions of service for this category of staff;
- the Swiss decree of 1966 which deals with working hours and weekly leave for editorial staff on newspapers and periodicals.

Other regulations concern journalists with a particular status. For example:
- a 1975 decree in the United Republic of Cameroon gives a particular status to civil servants in information departments (film producers, journalists, press secretaries and clerks) and deals with the recruitment and promotion of these officials;
- these same questions were the object of a decree issued in the Congo in 1975 which fixes the general status of the staff working in information services; [2]
- in the Gambia, official journalists come under the regulations of the public service;
- conditions of employment in the so-called "socialist" sector in Iraq (as opposed to the private sector) are determined through specific statutes and regulations;
- in the Libyan Arab Jamahiriya, accredited journalists (55 per cent) come under the law of 1956 on public service, while journalists paid by the day (34 per cent) are covered by the Labour Code of 1970 and those on contracts (11 per cent) fall under a regulation dated 1971 which applies to this type of staff.

Alongside this legislative and regulatory apparatus, professional organisations in most countries negotiate collective agreements, either on a national level or within the press groups. Detailed information on the contents of these agreements can be found in the following chapters. It is enough to mention at this point that some countries do not benefit from such agreements: the United Republic of Cameroon (public sector), Costa Rica, the Gambia, Honduras, Hong Kong, Kuwait, the Libyan Arab Jamahiriya and Madagascar.

The practice of individual contracts for journalists is not universally adopted. It is the rule for all journalists in Costa Rica and Poland, for journalists in the private sector in the United Republic of Cameroon and Iraq, and for journalists in establishments not covered by collective agreements in Denmark and in those not included in the decree on employment in Hong Kong. In Brazil, it is reserved for the top ranks in the hierarchy or in certain fields, such as sport. In Costa Rica, the contract is simply a verbal agreement. In France, it takes the form of a letter of engagement which is obligatory under the terms of the national collective agreement and which specifies the employment and professional qualifications of the person concerned, the appropriate collective agreement, the reference code, the effective starting date, the salary and the place of work. The letter of engagement is also the rule in the United Kingdom by virtue of the Contracts of Employment Act, 1972. In certain countries, there are particular types of individual contracts, as, for example, in the Federal Republic of Germany for editors on daily newspapers, or in Denmark, and also, of course, in many establishments in other countries.

Notes

[1] The law has been modified several times and notably by an amendment in 1979 which gives the Central Government authority to establish a tribunal when it considers that the Wage Board has not been functioning effectively.

[2] It is interesting to add that in the Congo the Department of Information, which controls journalists, is managed like all the other administrative units on the principle of tripartite decision-making *(trilogie déterminante)*: a tripartite body, consisting of representatives of management, trade unions and the party, takes all decisions relevant to the unit.

STRUCTURE OF THE PROFESSION 1

The profession of journalism is better structured than a casual outside observer would imagine and its practice complies with a set of rules laid down with different degrees of precision depending upon the country in question. However, it would appear to be infinitely variable if considered from the standpoint of the range of jobs and training to be found among journalists. The profession is particularly difficult to define in view of the fact that journalists often have a number of jobs and secondary activities.

RANGE OF DEFINITIONS IN THE PROFESSION

The expression "journalist" is often used in a very wide sense and includes those who contribute to newspapers only occasionally or rarely. It would obviously not be applied to novelists, university professors or politicians who might contribute articles from time to time, with or without a fee, outside their normal activities. But there are more ambiguous cases. For example, should the local correspondent of a newspaper, whose main revenue comes from another source, be considered as a journalist, even when paid by the newspaper?

When it is a matter of dealing with employment and working conditions, a more precise idea of the type of activity is needed. Legislators and professional organisations have formulated definitions in this respect.

Thus the statutes [1] for professional journalists in Argentina accord the title of journalist to persons who regularly perform, for pay, the jobs required in daily or periodical publications and in news agencies. Also included are those who perform these jobs in radio-broadcasting companies and in cinematic or television groups which distribute, project or televise information or news of a journalistic nature. Excluded are advertising agents and occasional collaborators or those outside the profession.

Profession: Journalist

To become an accredited journalist in Belgium, it is necessary: [2] (1) to be at least 21 years of age; (2) not to be deprived of rights under certain articles of the penal code; (3) to have practised as a main and habitual activity, for at least two years, the profession of journalism, i.e., to have participated in the editing of newspapers (daily or periodical), radio or television information programmes, cinema news programmes, or press agency material providing general information; (4) not to carry out any form of commercial activity and, in particular, any activity connected with advertising.

In France,[3] the professional journalist is "a person whose principal occupation, carried on regularly and for remuneration, is the exercise of his profession for a daily newspaper or a periodical ... and who derives his livelihood mainly from this occupation". A correspondent is "a professional journalist if he receives a fixed salary and fulfils the conditions laid down (above)". Also included in the bracket of professional journalists are "persons employed in direct connection with editorial work, viz., translators, shorthand reporters, sub-editors, cartoonists, press photographers (but not advertising agents or persons who are merely occasional collaborators ...) ...".

These three national definitions — taken from many others — have several points in common. First, journalism must be a regular, if not the principal, occupation of the person concerned. Thus, occasional or marginal collaborators, and in particular those who earn their principal living from another profession, are excluded. Next, this occupation must be exercised for payment, thus leaving aside unpaid contributors who are already excluded in any case because they contribute only occasionally and seek something other than a living from journalism. Moreover, these definitions do not confine the title of journalist to those who write for newspapers, since they also mention news agencies and, in the case of Argentina and Belgium, radio, television and cinema. Mention of the cinema no longer has much importance, since cinema news programmes have gone out of fashion. However, it is important to include in the profession of journalism those who prepare and present information bulletins and radio and television news programmes. It is also interesting to note that advertising agents are excluded.

Apart from the last point, the common features which have been noted above can also be found in the most recent version of the preamble to the model contract of the International Federation of Journalists (IFJ)[4] in which the professional journalist is considered to be every person whose main, regular and remunerated activity consists in contributing, by word or picture, to one or several written or audio-visual mass media and who derives most of his or her income from it. It will be noted that this version differs from the preceding one inasmuch as the model contract up to that time covered "journalists engaged on a permanent basis": this was a narrow definition which excluded "stringers", or collaborators paid by the line according to their production. There are a certain number of disadvantages in the situation of the stringer and it is understandable that the IFJ sought to improve it through this amendment. It will be noted moreover that the three national definitions quoted above contain nothing to exclude stringers as such.

In the *International standard classification of occupations* the status of the worker is left aside and only the jobs are described. A journalist is one who "collects, reports and comments on news and current affairs for publication in newspapers and periodicals or broadcasting by radio or television".[5] A more precise description of the functions of various categories of journalists is given later in this study. For the moment it is sufficient to keep to a brief description, based on the preceding definitions which state that these jobs should be carried out regularly for payment, that they should provide the main source of revenue for the person concerned and that they should be performed in the area of the written or audio-visual press or in a news agency.

If the regulations giving access to the profession in many countries are considered, a more precise definition of the journalist is required. It can be said that to wish to be a journalist does not make you one. Access to the profession is controlled in numerous places; the title of professional journalist is recognised and protected by law or by the profession itself and this, in turn, leads to a certain number of practical guarantees and advantages, but also to various obligations, particularly on the ethical level.

In a number of countries, recognition of the status is granted by a special organisation through registration on a professional register and the issue of a card. In Argentina,[6] inscription on the national register of journalists is compulsory and is granted without restrictions to persons who conform to the definition quoted above; it is certified by the issue of a professional card which serves as a pass, opens the doors to all sources of public interest information, to railway stations, airports, ports, etc., and allows the holder rebates on certain public service charges. Similarly, in Belgium, the law recognises and protects the status of professional journalist; a national press card, a pass and special car licence plates are supplied under this arrangement; a special committee, known as the "approval committee" *(agréation)*, decides on candidates. In Brazil, practice of the profession requires previous registration with the Ministry of Labour. In Costa Rica, journalists are grouped into a professional college which decides on admission according to standards established by legislation. In France, an identity card allowing access to certain administrative facilities is delivered by a body composed of seven newspaper directors and seven journalists, known as the *Commission de la carte d'identité des journalistes professionnels* (Identity Card Committee for Professional Journalists). A similar committee is also to be found in Madagascar and it consists of seven members: two government representatives, two members elected by and from newspaper and agency directors, and three members elected by and from journalists. In Italy, the Council of the Institute of Journalists, among other functions, decides on who should be registered on the register of journalists. In Luxembourg, a press council, composed equally of representatives of the press and of journalists, decrees on the existence or possible absence of conditions for the granting of a right to practise as a journalist and delivers the documents and identity passes.[7] There are two professional registers in Switzerland: one, managed by a joint committee of the Swiss Federation of Journalists and the Swiss Association of Newspaper Publishers, is concerned with the written press; the other deals with radio and television journalists.

The purpose of these different types of registration is obviously to encourage professionalism: the need for candidates to meet certain conditions and to maintain them after admission is calculated to exclude amateurs and to maintain high professional standards on the level of both technical qualifications and standards of behaviour. It is also interesting to note the attitude adopted by the Royal Commission on the Press in the United Kingdom with regard to a proposition submitted to it by the Institute of Journalists (IOJ) that a similar system of registration should be established. In the eyes of the IOJ, registration would be designed to raise standards of journalism in the public interest, to establish disciplinary procedures and to protect the employment of professional journalists, without putting the traditional freedom of the press at risk. The Commission did not give its approval to this proposition on the grounds that the obligation to be registered would create barriers to entering the profession and that exclusion from the register for disciplinary reasons would gravely compromise the chances of the journalists concerned in finding employment; moreover, this disciplinary aspect of registration would unduly load the already heavy arsenal of existing procedures in this sector.[8]

The effective practice of journalism thus varies from country to country, depending on whether more importance is attached to the need to organise the profession or to preserve free access to it, the latter being regarded as one of the elements of freedom of the press.

Professional status

From the definitions given above, it follows that journalists, in order to be recognised in their profession, must carry out their activity regularly and for payment. They can do this either as employees or as independent journalists.

As an employee of a section of the press (daily or other periodical, news agency, information service of a radio or television station), the

Structure of the profession

journalist will be bound by a contract, written or not, individual or otherwise, and will benefit from the conditions of employment stipulated in this contract. Generally speaking, these conditions are standard for persons in the same professional category, specifically in terms of job security, salary levels, hours of work, leave and social benefits. Most journalists work in the private sector. However, large numbers are also employed by a public or semi-public body and, in this context, are subject to special regulations: this is the case for journalists attached to certain radio and television networks where activity in a public service enterprise involves certain restrictions as well as certain advantages. Occasionally, journalists are no more than civil servants, either because they are attached to a press service within the administration or because all journalists in the country — or most of them, as in the Gambia and the Congo — are state employees.

Independent journalist, stringer, freelance, local correspondent — these are some of the terms used to describe the situation of journalists who, either directly or through an agency, offer their services for a specific product (an article, illustration, photograph or broadcast) for an amount to be agreed, or seek to sell a finished piece of work to a newspaper. They are different from the casual worker who may be directly employed by a news service on an irregular basis, acting as a replacement for example. The independent journalist may contribute regularly to one or several newspapers simultaneously and thus, while retaining independent status, may be occupied full time. In this way the advantage of regular and adequate pay is combined with the preservation of freedom, including freedom of expression, provided that this does not come into conflict with the policy followed by the newspapers concerned. But this dual advantage is by no means assured. Moreover, the situation of the independent journalist has a number of disadvantages, as is made clear by an investigation carried out in 1977 by the International Federation of Journalists.[9] According to this inquiry, this type of journalist sometimes has problems in obtaining a press card. Only in a few countries is the matter of their remuneration settled in a satisfactory way, since the existing provisions on this point hardly go beyond minimum fees and the laws relating to questions on author's rights. In practice, the income of independent journalists varies considerably depending on their ability to negotiate and, in this context, on their standing, as well as on the financial resources of the newspaper concerned: novice stringers are often poorly paid until their talents are recognised. Independent journalists are generally worse off in terms of social security than their colleagues in regular employment. In particular, in most countries they are not protected from the results of concentration of ownership in the press.

In brief, the problems facing independent workers in general are also to be found among independent journalists. It is true that they are attenuated in many countries through the existence of special legislative

Profession: Journalist

measures [10] or through the intervention of trade unions, which have opened their doors to journalists as well as others so as to give them some protection. The problems are, nevertheless, serious and are even more so by virtue of the fact that they affect a considerable percentage of the total number of journalists. To be more precise, there are some 350 independent journalists in Austria, 150 in Belgium, 300 to 400 in Denmark, 350 in Finland, 1,400 in France, 200 in Norway, 500 in Sweden, 480 in Switzerland and 3,000 in the United Kingdom.

Types of employer

A distinction has been drawn above between four different branches of the press.

The first two, namely, daily newspapers and other periodicals, are characterised by differences in publication frequency and, as a result, by the kind of information published: "hot" news in the first case and news presentation and commentary, somewhat later, in the second. Thus, the approach is different for the journalist. In both cases strict planning is necessary to meet deadlines, but staff on weekly or monthly publications obviously have more time for research and reflection and are exposed less than their colleagues on daily newspapers to the high tension that builds up before the rotary machines start to turn. It is, nevertheless, not unusual for a journalist to work simultaneously for both types of publication.

As for news agencies, their function is to find information and to sell it to their clients, who are principally newspapers and radio and television stations. Speed, reliability, objectivity and world-wide coverage are the essential attributes of their product.[11] These demands call for certain specific qualities in the journalists employed by news agencies — agency reporters. On the professional level, they must be capable of sifting the news, checking it and presenting it lucidly and concisely. The news agency is therefore a hard school where numerous journalists acquire their skills and experience. Staffs of news agencies are considerable, particularly where the major international agencies are concerned: in 1976, Agence France-Press (AFP) employed 954 journalists and correspondents and 1,422 stringers and contributors;[12] Associated Press (AP) had 2,500 journalists and photographers and 600 to 700 stringers overseas; United Press (UP) had more than 2,000 journalists; Reuters had 500 journalists and 800 stringers and contributors; and Tass employed 2,000 collaborators.[13] The big news agencies operate round the clock, thus requiring many of their staff to work inconvenient hours. News agencies are at the mercy of the time factor and have been quick to profit from the advantages of computers. This, in turn, has produced the human problems for staff which inevitably go with the introduction of computers.

Structure of the profession

Table 1. Distribution of journalists among the information media in selected countries (in actual numbers or percentages)

Country	Dailies	Other publications	Agencies	Radio/TV
Australia (1976/77)	2 392	+	120	700
Austria (1976)	12%	17%	10%	12%
Belgium (1974)	1 100	150	+	206
Denmark (1976)	1 520	194	+	346
France (1964-71)	42%	26%	7%	9%
Ghana (1978)	50%	5%	20%	25%
Italy (1977)	3 718	676	487	915
New Zealand (1971)		1 524	16	196
New Zealand (1978)				335
Poland (1979)	2 050	1 708	442	1 000
Sweden (1976)	4 275	812	+	778

+ Unknown.
Source. Replies to an ILO questionnaire, 1978; for Austria: *Massen-Medien in Österreich* (Vienna, Internationale Publikationen Gesellschaft, 1977); for Belgium: International Federation of Journalists; for France: Study and Research Centre on Qualifications (CEREQ).

Radio and television information services — the fourth type under examination in this study — are also subject to a number of specific restrictions. The news bulletins they put out are generally somewhat short; in fact, the text of a normal televised news programme would fill only a few columns in a daily newspaper. A choice has to be made as to which events to report and the style of presentation represents a different journalistic technique from that used in the newspaper world. Radio journalism and television journalism — themselves different in several respects — thus require specific qualifications. However, the pace of work is comparable to that used in the production of a daily newspaper: written, spoken or televised, the news report has its inexorable deadlines and thus makes the same stern demands on the editorial rooms. Similarly, the preparation of a weekly or monthly magazine and that of a radio or television journal have many points in common from the journalist's point of view.

Statistical data on the spread of journalists between these various media are limited. Table 1 offers a partial picture which, while not allowing a comparison to be made on the international level, provides an idea of the relative breakdown of staff employed in the four information media in selected countries. The printed press is naturally the largest employer. But despite the differences in the techniques used by the media, there is no watertight division and there are large numbers of journalists who place their talents, successively or simultaneously, at the disposal of one or other of the media.

Profession: Journalist

VARIETY OF FUNCTIONS

The infinite variety of the press and the subjects it handles is naturally reflected in a whole range of specialities among journalists: politics, economics, social affairs, law, arts, philosophy, science and technology, sport, gastronomy, news items, etc. — in fact, a mirror of the numerous aspects of human activity. But when these specialities are looked at across the board, a certain number of functions can be defined. These are shared among journalists and effectively determine their ranking in the hierarchy. Several countries, such as Australia and the United Republic of Cameroon, group them into a small number of grades or "classes", but most others recognise a range of titles covering activities which are more or less identical from one country to another. The range can sometimes be extremely wide: for example, the agreement used by the French regional dailies has no less than 30 definitions, from chief editor to press cartoonist.

This is no place to describe the various functions in detail, but it is worth dwelling on three of them which, with slight variations, are common to all important newspapers: editor, sub-editor and reporter. To these can be added, since the title is peculiar to the branch, that of radio and television journalist. For these four functions, especially the last two, the journalist may be a specialist in a particular field and may be named accordingly.

Editor

According to the *International standard classification of occupations*,[14] the editor "selects, revises and arranges material for publication in newspapers and periodicals". He or she "allots assignments to reporters, correspondents and photographers; appraises reports, commentaries and photographs submitted and selects them for publication; assigns writing of editorials and leading articles to specialist writers; examines material for conformity with established policy and literary standards of publisher and revises it as necessary; decides spacing and positioning of items to be included, writes headlines and instructs printer concerning kinds of type to be used". The editor may also be called upon "to write articles or columns".

The editor is therefore a key person whose decisions dictate the contents and look of each edition. However, the position of editor can be ambiguous because of a dual obligation: on the one hand, to the editorial team which he or she organises and directs; and, on the other hand, through the management functions of the job, to the employer (that is, the owner of the newspaper or the owner's director-representative). The ambiguity is such that the position of editor is not

Structure of the profession

always understood where the application of collective agreements or pay scales is concerned. To maintain independence from the two sides is no easy task, as can be seen from the recent history of various newspapers. This is a problem which has taxed the brains of various groups. For example, the Commission which from 1974 to 1977 studied the problems of the press in the United Kingdom stated that the independence of the editor could not be guaranteed unless certain fundamental rights were respected: [15]

— the right to reject editorial material supplied by the central management or editorial services;
— the right to decide on the contents of the newspaper (within reasonable economic limits and within the policy established for the publication);
— the right to authorise expenses within the agreed budget;
— the right to carry out investigative journalism;
— the right to reject advice on editorial policy;
— the right to criticise the group to which the newspaper belongs or other elements in the same group;
— the right to change the position of the newspaper on specific problems, while following the general agreed line;
— the right to hire or fire journalists, to fix the terms of their employment contracts within the context of the established policy of the group and to assign jobs to them.

Conferences with department heads or columnists, editorial work (the editorial is often the direct responsibility of the editor), discussions, management duties, and social obligations make the job an extremely busy one. The editor is usually aided by a deputy editor and some of the functions of the job are delegated to specialists, at least on the major newspapers.[16]

Sub-editor

Again according to the *International standard classification of occupations*,[17] the sub-editor "assists with editing of newspapers, magazines, trade journals and other publications; edits copy for spelling, punctuation, grammar and continuity; verifies factual content of articles using standard reference sources; rewrites articles for greater consistency, clarity and adherence to space limitations; prepares layout of pages showing position and sizes of illustrations; reads unsolicited manuscripts and selects those for review by editor; drafts headlines and captions; replies to correspondence concerning publication matters".

In large newspapers, a deputy editor, aided by the chief sub-editor, directs and co-ordinates the work described above. This person is ultimately responsible for the production of the newspaper, under the direction of the editor, and is responsible for make-up and scheduling in particular.

The news-room is in many ways a demanding place. The journalists who work there must be all-round performers, with a sharp news sense, a sound journalistic style, a mastery of language, a solid general culture and a good understanding of the laws governing the press. Just as essential are technicians who are capable of giving prominence to the events of the day through their knowledge of make-up techniques, arrangement of headlines, and choice of type-faces and illustrations. Journalists must also be able to work at all hours of the day and night, no matter how inconvenient. Morning newspapers require their editorial staff to work from 5 or 6 o'clock in the evening until 1 o'clock in the morning, and even later if a news flash breaks in the middle of the night.[18]

Reporter

According to the *International standard classification of occupations*,[19] the reporter "seeks and reports information of interest to the public for publication in newspapers; travels to scene of assignment, such as a reported crime, a trial, a fire, an accident, an important public function, a sports meeting or a fashion show; collects all available information concerning assignment by observation, interview and investigation, seeking especially information on aspects of subject likely to interest newspaper readers; writes reports based on information collected and submits them to editorial department for approval and preparation for publication".

The reporter is often accompanied on outside assignments by a news photographer who "takes photographs to illustrate stories and articles for publication in newspapers, magazines and similar journals . . . specialises in travelling on assignments to photograph people and events of current public interest".[20] At times the reporters themselves take the photographs to illustrate their articles; this is often the case with local correspondents who send their own stories and photos to the newspaper. Conversely, the news photographer may carry out pictorial news assignments alone. This could be the case for those working on behalf of photo agencies or the picture department of a major news agency.

Apart from the technical qualifications necessary for the job, the reporter and the news photographer must have a highly developed sense of initiative and flexibility. Whether acting on an order or of their own free will, they must be ready at any moment to go to the spot where the event is happening, even if it offers no hope of bringing off the "scoop" that every ambitious journalist dreams about. They must also accept

Structure of the profession

irregular hours of work. The news-room of a big daily newspaper operates under the same kind of high pressure as the major news agencies and reporters are moving in and out continuously. For them, perhaps more than for any other journalist, the concept of fixed working hours is meaningless.[21]

Radio and television journalist

According to the description given in the *International standard classification of occupations*,[22] the radio and television journalist "performs tasks similar to those of a journalist ... but specialises in preparing and broadcasting reports and commentaries over radio and television, conducts 'live' interviews with persons knowledgeable on or involved in events of current interest".

Apart from the interview, these activities are similar to those carried out by journalists of the printed press; they thus require the same basic qualifications. However, they are different in terms of expression and, on this account, they call for additional qualities. For example, the art of speaking in public and the ability to adjust oneself immediately according to the reactions of the person being interviewed. Journalists who contribute to the preparation of radio and television news transmissions, without speaking into the microphone or appearing before the camera, must also adapt their material to this medium. Writing for radio and writing for print are two different things; and writing for sound is quite a different thing from writing for the visual medium.[23]

The numerical breakdown of the four categories mentioned above cannot really be determined. There are obviously only a small number of editors, but sub-editors and reporters certainly make up the large body of the press. To take just one example, these two groups together represent 61 per cent of the editorial staff on the British national press.[24] Table 1 gives some idea of the number of radio and television journalists in selected countries; the number is probably constantly increasing, if the case of New Zealand is anything to go by.

RANGE OF TRAINING

Initial training

Journalists have very varied backgrounds and forms of training. Generally speaking, the profession is becoming more and more technical and now demands more training than formerly.

For many years, the art of reporting current events in a lively fashion was the primary quality required of a good journalist. It was generally considered that literary talent was innate, that it developed naturally but could not be acquired. That is why there was, and is, a saying that "journalists are born and not made". This statement would appear to be exaggerated today. Writing talent is still indispensable but it must now go hand in hand with a wide-ranging intellect, or with expertise in a specific field, but preferably with both. The average reader's level of knowledge and appetite for information have increased. As a result, people expect their newspapers to inform them on all aspects of human activity. Thus, the editorial team must include specialists in the main branches of the humanities and the social sciences who must be capable of explaining in clear language to their readers the current developments in politics, economics, social affairs, science, the arts, etc.

That is why the background for a journalist must first and foremost be one of a solid general culture, completed in most cases by specialisation in a particular area. How can this cultural background and specialisation be acquired and what level is required? The situation varies considerably from one country to another and it would need a whole book to describe it.

As has been seen, practice of the profession demands an increasing level of qualification. There is a general impression that the average level of knowledge among journalists is going up from one generation to another, although this may be due to other factors which have no bearing on the requirements of the profession as such — for example, the average level of education in society as a whole, or the limitation of access to the profession which may result in the average candidate being overqualified. Whatever the case, it would seem that the self-taught person or the copy boy who becomes a reporter is an increasingly rare sight in news-rooms. They will become even rarer as the old guard disappears little by little and, as will be seen later on, as certain regulations impose conditions of access to the profession which stipulate a specific level of education.

Statistics and especially chronological data are not available to support the impression that the level of instruction is gradually going up. Figures gathered by the National Council for the Training of Journalists in the United Kingdom relating to the level of instruction of young journalists in the early phase of their training under the auspices of this Council from 1964 to 1975 are, however, revealing (table 2). They show a regular and substantial reduction in the percentage of poorly educated trainees and naturally a corresponding increase in the percentage of the better educated.

Data on three other countries, while not showing the same evolution, at least provide a general idea of the situation in relatively recent years.

An inquiry [25] carried out in Austria in 1974 by the Institute of Social Research, on behalf of the Federal Ministry of Social Administration,

Structure of the profession

Table 2. United Kingdom: Educational level of reporters under training, 1964-75 (in percentages)

	GCE [1] "O" Level (fewer than five subjects)	GCE [1] "O" Level (five or more subjects)	GCE [1] "A" Level (one or more subjects)	University degree
1964	32	35	29	4
1965	25	35	35	5
1966	27	32	35	6
1967	23	30	38	9
1968	17	33	35	15
1969	–	–	–	–
1970	6	25	50	20
1971	4	21	59	15
1972	2	21	60	14
1973	3	21	58	16
1974	2	17	60	17
1975	1	13	61	22

– Data not available.
[1] General Certificate of Education. Ordinary level ("O") represents four years of secondary studies; Advanced level ("A") represents an additional two years.
Source. National Council for the Training of Journalists, in Royal Commission on the Press: *Final report. Appendices* (London, HMSO, 1977), p. 150.

revealed the following results: about one-quarter of the persons interviewed had a university degree; another quarter had studied at university but had not gained a degree; another quarter had completed high school studies (general and technical); 18 per cent had attended high school but had not graduated with a certificate *(Matura)*; and 6 per cent had simply completed the minimum schooling required by law. Among those who had followed university courses, 36 per cent had studied philosophy, history or psychology, 19 per cent law or Germanic culture, 11 per cent journalism and 36 per cent other subjects. In contrast with these figures, 53 per cent of the persons interviewed felt that special professional training was necessary for journalists, 62 per cent preferred training on the job, 32 per cent wanted to see schools of journalism set up, 14 per cent opted for the study of journalism and mass communications at university, 14 per cent opted for other study areas and 14 per cent opted for advanced professional training.

Another investigation,[26] carried out in France, at the request of the Ministry of Education, by the Centre for Studies and Research on Qualifications (CEREQ), concerned journalists who had entered the profession between 1964 and 1971. It emerged that 21 per cent of journalists held high school diplomas, 23 per cent had completed one or two years of high school studies, 25 per cent had obtained the high school certificate *(baccalauréat)* or completed their high school technical studies, 25 per cent had attended high school without obtaining the *baccalauréat* and 7 per cent had completed only primary school education. It will be noted that these figures are more or less similar to those which were produced by the Austrian inquiry. The General Union of Journalists, affiliated to the *Force ouvrière (Syndicat général des journalistes/Force ouvrière)* estimates that the proportion of journalists who failed to follow studies leading to the *baccalauréat*, and the percentage of those who did not complete their high school studies, has decreased since the CEREQ inquiry, which means that the proportion of diplomas at intermediary and advanced levels has increased. It is worth pointing out that, according to the same inquiry, former pupils of specialised schools of journalism choose the news-room or the publishing department, or editorial or reporting jobs, rather than technical positions (make-up for example) or positions of responsibility. The inquiry also reveals the small numbers of former students of technical subjects who go through schools of journalism, as well as the significant proportion — to be expected, perhaps — of journalists with technical jobs who emerge from technical centres.

Statistical data on Sweden dating from 1969 shows that 8 per cent of male journalists then held a university degree, 27 per cent had passed the upper secondary school qualification *(abiture)* and 65 per cent had not reached a high-school level of education. The corresponding figures for female journalists were 12, 44 and 44 per cent.[27]

The range of university studies followed by Austrian journalists is probably fairly representative of the situation in other countries. The study of literature, philosophy, history and law is a good basis on which to build the indispensable cultural foundation, and many of the current famous names in the press started in that way. Among journalists in the specialised press, however, are many former students of faculties of economics and science.

The teaching of journalism as such at universities is a relatively recent development. Moreover, the way in which it is taught varies from one country to another and even from one university to another.[28] Broadly speaking, it is considered either as the study of modern society or as a form of professional training. In the first case, study is focused on the theory of communications and the interaction of communications with other aspects of society; in the second case, the techniques of journalism are studied. Between these two extremes is a whole range of approaches which combine the academic and pragmatic approaches in various degrees.

At the risk of over-simplification, it can be said that in North America the pragmatic approach has predominated for a long time. Courses used to be focused on the practical side of the profession, but now the academic approach has found more favour at universities, because technical training can no longer match the rapid evolution in newspaper production techniques and because it is now preferable to equip students with an overall intellectual background which will enable them to handle any new situation. The example of the Graduate School of Journalism at Columbia University in the United States is evidence that the professional teaching of journalism still has its supporters. Its courses are concentrated on the printed and audio-visual press, as well as on ethical, political, economic, scientific and sociological problems, at national and international level. Students carry out investigations into current events with the help of professional journalists. The school has news-rooms, a radio studio, a teleprinter linked to the main news agencies and a specialised reference library, not to mention the libraries and computers at Columbia University itself. The effectiveness of the training is demonstrated by the fact that some 200 editors and 150 foreign correspondents have emerged from these courses and that, for example, the *New York Times* employs more than 70 graduates from this school.[29]

University facilities in Europe are so varied that they defy any generalisation. It can be said, however, that in Western Europe, university courses in journalism tend to be academic rather than practical and that the university is not the only, nor even the main, path to journalism. Yet in Austria, Belgium, Finland, France, the Federal Republic of Germany, Italy, Spain, Switzerland and the United Kingdom, there is at least one university which offers courses specially designed for would-be journalists. For example, in the Federal Republic of Germany, the universities of Berlin, Bochum, Bremen, Göttingen, Mainz, Munich, Munster and Erlangen-Nuremberg offer courses in public relations and communications which represent a form of preparatory professional training for journalism and other fields. The section for journalists in the programme of the Faculty of Information Sciences at the University of Madrid is obviously designed for press professionals. The International Centre for Advanced Training in Journalism at Strasbourg, which operates in collaboration with the city's university and with UNESCO, and whose appeal goes beyond Europe to reach out to Africa and the Middle East, is a centre for the study of matters related to the teaching of journalism.

The universities of Eastern Europe play a large role in the training of future journalists. This has been true in the USSR since the beginning of the twenties and there are now 24 universities with a Faculty of Journalism. In Czechoslovakia, the German Democratic Republic, Poland and Yugoslavia, the teaching of professional journalism was set up after the Second World War. In Poland, for example, there is a Faculty of Journalism at the universities of Warsaw, Kraków, Poznań, Katowice and Wroclaw. Academic teaching, research and practical training are blended together in these establishments on the basis of a formula which varies from country to country. The Faculty of Journalism at the State University of Lomonosov, in Moscow, is a good example of this mixture. It has nine chairs: theory and practice of the party press, radio and television, publishing, techniques of the press and mass media, history of journalism and Russian literature, history of the party press in the USSR, Russian stylistics, history of the press and history of world literature. It has a print shop, a newspaper made up by the students, radio and television studios, a typing and shorthand section and a photographic studio. The programme includes one year of apprenticeship with the press, radio and television.

After the independence of many countries in Africa, there was a rapid growth of institutions providing systematic teaching on the mass media and the universities played an increasingly important role in this area. In 1965, this type of university teaching could be found in only two countries, Egypt and Nigeria. Now it is also available in Algeria, the United Republic of Cameroon, Ghana, Kenya, the Libyan Arab Jamahiriya, Madagascar, Senegal, South Africa, Tunisia and Zaire. The need to place the trainees rapidly has had a dual effect: on the one hand, a shorter period of training; on the other, at least initially, the placing of emphasis on practical aspects of training rather than on academic studies and research.

In Asia, as well, the universities play a major role in teaching subjects related to the mass media. Examples of this are to be found in India, Indonesia, Japan, the Philippines and Thailand. In this region, as elsewhere, it is increasingly recognised that journalists must not only have a solid general culture but must also be introduced to the social sciences and that, for this, the university is the appropriate place. It is also felt that it is important to associate the universities with the achievement of national objectives and that, in this context, the training they provide must include technical and professional aspects. This approach is naturally applied to the teaching of journalism. However, on this point, the traditional idea of honour in Japan appears to distinguish that country from other countries: the specialised schools of journalism lean towards the academic; they are not regarded as a training ground for the profession; moreover, they do not provide privileged access to it, since the various sections of the press have their own training systems.

The links between university teaching and preparation for journalism seem somewhat remote in Australia where only one university — the University of Queensland — provides courses in this sector. In New Zealand, such courses are more common. Students with the University Entrance qualifications can follow preparatory courses at the Auckland Technical Institute or the Wellington Polytechnic. People with a university degree are admitted to the Diploma in Journalism at the University of Canterbury.

Most Latin American countries have at least one institution for training in journalism and the majority of these are associated with universities. Indeed, if taken as a whole, this is the region in which

Structure of the profession

universities are most closely involved with the profession. Some commentators have attributed this to the fact that the large number of opinion groups calls for a corresponding number of journalists and that the large number of universities allows this need to be met. Others feel that only a small proportion of students in journalism finally make a career in the profession, a fact which would appear to contradict the former explanation. In any event, the tendency to organise specialised professional training for journalists in Latin American universities is clearly evident, particularly in Argentina and Brazil where at least one-half of these training institutions are to be found. However, it is at the Central University of Quito where the International Centre for Higher Studies in Journalism for Latin America (CIESPAL) has been set up. This Centre has played a major part in raising the teaching level in journalism through the training of teachers, the supply of documentation to other institutions and research activities.

As can be seen from this brief survey, the teaching of journalism at universities or in institutions linked to them has many aspects and does not always guarantee — far from it — a training focused on the practice of the profession. This explains why certain countries have found it useful to plug the gaps in the system by creating specialised schools, usually set up outside the university sphere. Such schools exist, for example in Costa Rica, Denmark, France, the Federal Republic of Germany, India, Ireland, Poland, Sweden and Switzerland. They are similar in their methods, if not in their capacities, to the two great establishments mentioned above: the Columbia University Graduate School of Journalism and the Faculty of Journalism at the State University of Lomonosov.

Training within the profession

The teaching of journalism at universities or in specialised schools involves a considerable number of persons. However, not all of them become journalists; in fact, the proportion of those who enter the profession is difficult to determine. Conversely, many journalists — it is impossible to say exactly how many — have not passed through these establishments. Their training has taken a different route. Whether they started with another kind of university education or simply a high school grade, in all cases they will have had a fairly long and reasonably systematic apprenticeship in the trade with part of the press. Such an apprenticeship also often completes the training given in degree courses or in schools of journalism. In brief, whatever the level and nature of their previous education, most journalists have learned their trade "on the job" before they have earned the right to call themselves journalists. The saying that "journalists are born and not made" is certainly open to question.

Profession: Journalist

In many countries, whether through tradition, or through the lack or inadequacy of specialised training establishments or perhaps a certain scepticism on the part of the press as to their efficiency, or because of regulations resulting from legislation or collective agreements, training in the enterprise or under its guidance remains the normal way to enter the profession.

Thus, in the Federal Republic of Germany, about 90 per cent of journalists on daily newspapers acquired their training with newspapers over a two-year course during which they received only very modest pay. This high percentage would seem to be the result of university programmes which the profession criticises as too academic and lacking in specifics.[30] The course is drawn up according to directives established in 1968 by common agreement between the press and the trade unions for journalists.

In Argentina, under the terms of a law of 1946 regarding the status of the professional journalist (Law No. 12908, article 24), the proportion of "would-be candidates" to the number of journalists in employment must not exceed one-fifth or one-eighth, depending on the economic level of the publication. After two years of service, the candidate, if at least 20 years of age, must be incorporated into one of the professional categories defined by the law (for example, "reporter"). The collective agreement of 1975, which is applicable to publications in Buenos Aires, made it obligatory for press enterprises to set up professional training programmes (article 35).

In Australia, the courses in journalism given by advanced training institutions are generally considered by the press as only a useful basic background and entry into the profession is usually made at the "cadet" level. According to the 1974 labour law concerning metropolitan daily newspapers, a cadet is an employee who is under permanent or regular training in journalism, but is not yet classified as a "graded" journalist (article 10). Although there is no upper age limit, the majority of these cadets are 17 or 18 year olds who have obtained their Higher School Certificate or completed their fifth year of secondary school. They remain cadets for four years if they are 17 years of age and for three years if older. For those who have completed higher studies, the course is reduced to one year. The proportion of cadets to graded journalists is in the ratio of one to five. Those who have not followed a course of advanced studies are encouraged to do so and are granted leave for this purpose.

Under the terms of the national collective contract for journalists in the French press (article 10), the title of professional journalist is granted at the end of a recognised two-year course. The number of probationers cannot exceed 15 per cent of the total editorial staff. In practice, a press establishment may organise the courses as it pleases. An agreement with one press establishment stipulates that, following a trial period of three months, the probationer journalist must be trained

Structure of the profession

successively in editorial and make-up work and then in a department which will not be his or her final place of assignment. With the news agencies, this apprenticeship is naturally made at the news desk, whatever diploma is held by the probationer.[31] As has been mentioned earlier, this is an excellent training ground, not only for working inside the agency but also for any career in journalism.

In Italy, the law of 1963, which regulates the profession of journalism, provides for a register of trainees in addition to the register of journalists mentioned earlier. Persons of 18 years of age and over can be entered on this register after a test in general culture, although this test is waived for those who hold certain diplomas. A trainee cannot remain on this register for more than three years (articles 33-34). The national collective agreement stipulates certain conditions for the number of trainees. For example, the numerical proportion must be one trainee to every ten, or fraction of ten, reporters in news-rooms employing up to 100 editorial staff; and one trainee to every 25, or fractions of 25, reporters in news-rooms with more than 100 editorial staff. The trial period must not exceed three months. The trainee is entitled to a prescribed minimum salary, a thirteenth month, payment for overtime, and annual leave of 20 working days, etc., and the duration of the training course is taken into consideration in calculating length of service.

In Japan, where the press hires staff from among students leaving university or through competitive examinations organised by them, initial training is given to the recruits in courses that can last from one week to four months, depending on the establishment.

In Liberia, there is no teaching institute for journalism, and training is done exclusively on the job. Neither the three newspapers nor the two radio stations do this systematically. Future journalists are generally recruited at the end of their high school studies and learn the profession by practising it.[32]

One daily newspaper in Nigeria has its own training centre which has adequate staff and equipment. It provides courses in reporting, photography, etc., and, although dependent on a newspaper, is unique inasmuch as it opens its doors to other media and also awards diplomas.[33]

The distinction made in Australia between cadets and graded journalists is also found in New Zealand. There, the arbitration clauses for the profession oblige employers to give cadets a sound training. This must take place during working hours and is carried out with the technical aid of the Journalist Training Board, one of 28 Industry Training Boards created by law in 1972 (Vocational Training Council Amendment Act, No. 113). In addition to formal courses, the training includes revision of copy edited by the cadets and reporting assignments with graded journalists. Cadets are granted six hours a week, without loss of pay, to follow outside courses. All cadets who have worked for two years continuously and who have a shorthand speed of 80 words/minute are promoted to the rank of first-year journalist (see Chapter 5). A working period of three years and a shorthand speed of 120 words/minute leads to their promotion to the rank of second-year journalist. The number of cadets must not exceed one-quarter of the combined total of graded journalists and cadets.[34]

In the United Kingdom, the training of candidates for the profession of journalist is carried out mainly under the auspices of the newspapers themselves. Traditionally it is the provincial press which plays this role and which thus acts as a recruiting ground for national newspapers.[35] Training is supervised by the National Council for the Training of Journalists (NCTJ).

Basic training takes two forms: direct entry as an apprentice, or preparatory courses (before hiring as such) for a period of one year, followed by a shortened period of apprenticeship. Direct apprenticeship is chosen by most of the candidates who become journalists on daily newspapers and the training is carried out in the news-rooms. External courses complete this training. A Proficiency Certificate is awarded at the end of the course by the NCTJ, but is not compulsory. Many probationers abstain from the tests on the grounds that they are not a satisfactory way of evaluating professional qualifications. It is not essential to pass the examination, or even to take it, in order to become a "graded journalist". In the absence of a certificate, this status becomes automatic following a certain period of employment, which varies according to age and the type of training received. Similarly, the title of "fully qualified journalist", which also figures in collective agreements, is not dependent upon the holding of a certificate. This title is granted to journalists with at least two-and-a-half years' continuous experience on a full-time basis, of which the last 12 months must have been in the service of a daily newspaper or national news agency. Preparatory courses are on a full-time basis and are given at tertiary-level colleges at the Centre for Journalism Studies at University College in Cardiff and at the City University of London. The students in these colleges are either sponsored by their future employers or are self-supporting and selected on the basis of interviews with the NCTJ. Certain aspects of the training are regulated by collective agreements. Special clauses stipulate the salaries of trainees, including students sponsored from the preparatory courses. Others deal with the length of training which varies from one-and-a-half to three years, based on how much preliminary training the students have had. Other clauses concern the acceptable proportion of trainees within the total staff. This is defined either in general terms (for example, the numbers must be such as to allow graded journalists the time to devote adequate attention to trainees and to allow the latter to follow the courses), or in precise figures (for example, the number of probationers in a news agency must

Structure of the profession

not exceed 10 per cent of the combined total of reporters and sub-editors).

In the French-speaking part of Switzerland, candidates in journalism go through a two-year course of training during which they work in the main editorial service departments and follow a programme of group and individual study established by a commission for professional and continuous training chosen jointly by the Newspaper Union of French-speaking Switzerland and the Swiss Federation of Journalists.

It should be noted that certain broadcasting groups have their own training systems which are designed for journalists only or for all programme staff. Thus, in the Federal Republic of Germany, the radio and television network *(Westdeutscher Rundfunk)* offers university graduates training contracts which last for 18 months. The network also accepts other students who want to sit in on the course, but for contracts of only two or three months. The Swedish radio provides a whole range of courses which are designed to train new recruits and add to the qualifications of staff already employed.

WORKING FOR MORE THAN ONE EMPLOYER

Quite often the same name appears in several newspapers or other publications. Equally, a newspaper journalist appears in other media or a television commentator takes part in a radio programme or writes for a publication. Anonymity or the use of a pen-name conceals this practice to some extent, but it is fairly widespread.

By virtue of their situation, stringers often work for several employers. In this respect, they are subject to the normal rules of competition, inasmuch as they cannot sell the same story to several newspapers in the same area of distribution. However, rules and actual practice hardly go beyond this basic principle.[36] In Sweden, however, if the contract guarantees the journalist a fixed minimum, the editor has the right to insist that he or she does not work for another employer. In Finland, some editors demand that the name of other employers be disclosed, but the journalist is free to refuse; in Luxembourg, however, the journalist cannot refuse. In France, the employer can ask professional journalists, employed on a casual basis, to be informed of their regular contributions to other journals; there is no precise ruling on whether they are obliged to give this information. In Switzerland, journalists are obliged to inform management, if so requested, of the various publications with which they collaborate on a regular basis and of those to which they have made, or intend to make, contributions. In the Federal Republic of Germany, when the sharing of professional expenses has been settled between the different employers of the same correspondent, the latter must obtain their consent before entering into new commitments and the expense sharing is then extended to the new employer.

But the problem is obviously more complicated when journalists are regular staff members of a newspaper and receive a salary from that newspaper rather than fees for occasional contributions. What motives might they have for making their services available to other news publications? Have they the right to do it? Should they be engaged in secondary activities?

The inadequacy of pay in a single job is given, among others, as the motive for working for more than one employer. Certain newspapers, because of their small circulation or for other economic reasons, are not able to offer all their contributors a decent wage. For example, the Costa Rican Government noted that multiple employment was a problem in the sixties and early seventies, but that the fixing of a minimum salary enabled many journalists to be satisfied with a single pay packet. It added, however, that there were still many cases of multiple employment, to the extent that certain sections of the press were concerned about conflicts of interest and, as a result, had prohibited their employees from working for other publications. In Spain, the State Federation for Information and the Graphic Arts feels that this is a serious problem. In addition to their normal employment, many journalists in that country occupy posts in public administration or in private enterprise in order to obtain a higher standard of living, thus barring young people from finding their first job in these sectors. The need for journalists to take on several jobs in order to meet their basic needs is also noted in Honduras.

There are other reasons, rarely mentioned but obvious, which explain why well-known journalists make occasional contributions to publications other than their own. One of them is the professional satisfaction felt by the journalists when their ideas are exposed to a new public and their talents are more widely appreciated. Another is the desire on the part of the newspaper concerned to acquire a star writer or occasionally to reinforce a limited editorial team. Yet again, the reputation of the principal employer is enhanced when the newspaper's contributors are sought by others. And finally, there is sometimes simply a shortage of certain specialists.

In any case, the practice of working for more than one employer and the habit of taking on additional assignments lead to a number of problems: a negative effect on a shrinking labour market (as noted in Spain), the danger of overwork and possible legal disputes between different press groups. This explains why many countries have established certain regulations on the question.[37]

In some countries, the accumulation of journalistic work, or the linking of journalism with other salaried activities, is forbidden, or at least not accepted in practice. In the United Republic of Cameroon and

Structure of the profession

Madagascar, it is regarded as incompatible with the definition of the profession of journalist or with the status of a civil servant, which is the situation of most journalists in these two countries. It is prohibited in Italy by law and by the work contract and in Japan through the tradition of loyalty to a single employer. There is a tacit rule in Denmark that journalists should abstain from any other salaried activity. The main target for this prohibition is often commercial activity and the prohibition is either direct or by way of a ban on promotional activities: this applies in Belgium, Greece, Luxembourg, Sweden, Turkey and the United Kingdom. Only in exceptional cases and on a temporary basis can a journalist in Israel engage in public relations or commercial press activities.

Elsewhere, it is possible to work for more than one employer within the profession. There is no ban or restriction in Austria, Brazil, Chile, Finland, Honduras, Hong Kong, India,[38] Iraq in the public sector, Kuwait, the Netherlands, Norway, Poland, Spain and the United States. In other countries, contributing to several papers is subject to certain conditions and restrictions. In Argentina, for example, a journalist can work "full time" for three newspapers simultaneously, and can thus receive three salaries. In Australia, where it is the custom for full-time journalists to work for only one employer, specialist column writers can work for other newspapers. Certain publishers in the State of Victoria can authorise their journalists to send copies of articles to other publishers for publication. In Barbados and Guyana, local journalists act as correspondents for foreign newspapers. In Canada, a collective agreement allows external collaboration outside normal working hours, on condition that the work is not offered to other media in the same distribution area (unless by special permission), that it is first offered to the employer and that, if the journalist appears on radio or television, the newspaper he or she works for is mentioned.

The national collective agreement in France stipulates that outside collaboration by professional journalists employed full or part time must be notified in advance in writing to the employer who reserves the right to refuse permission, provided that reasons can be given for this decision. Similar arrangements exist in the collective agreement in Senegal. The authorisation of the publisher is also required in Ireland and Pakistan. In Malaysia, one of the newspaper groups allows its editorial staff reasonable freedom to collaborate with other publications, outside normal working hours, but attaches a number of conditions which effectively limit its application. In New Zealand, where almost all journalists work full time for one employer, some of them offer articles written in their spare time to other publications. If a publishing house has several publications, journalists who are members of the New Zealand Journalists Union work for only one of them. Under the terms of the collective agreement in Switzerland, reporters must devote all their normal working hours to the publication which employs them. However, outside these prescribed working hours, and provided that their work and the interests of the publication are not adversely affected, they may collaborate with other media if their work contracts do not expressly prevent this and on condition that they obtain the agreement of their publisher. A similar restriction in the work contract applies in the private sector in Iraq. The Tunisian Labour Code [39] stipulates that the right to have articles published in different publications is subject to a specific agreement which indicates the circumstances under which the reproduction may be authorised.

Two radio-television networks in the Federal Republic of Germany have set out guide-lines on the subject. They stipulate that there must be prior management approval, that employees cannot act as editor for another news medium and that they are obliged to reveal any possible pseudonyms to management, to give first refusal of their material to management and to conduct themselves in such a manner as to avoid giving the impression that they are members of the editorial team of the outside publication. The Swedish radio insists on advance approval, amongst other obligations.

In a third group of countries, dual employment is possible in activities outside the profession. The exercise of these activities is not subject to any formal rules in Austria, Finland, the Netherlands, Norway and the United States. In other countries, such activities are subject to certain restrictions. In Argentina, employment on a newspaper is incompatible with employment in the civil service or in a company which is licensed to act in the public service sector. A collective agreement in Canada excludes secondary activities which are visibly in conflict with the responsibilities and duties of the employee or which involve competition with the employee's publication. A group of Malaysian publications stipulates that external activities must not affect the physical and mental health of the person concerned. The Code of Professional Conduct of the National Union of Journalists in Ireland is more specific and restrictive: "A member holding a staff appointment shall serve first the paper that employs him. In his own time a member is free to engage in other creative work but he should not undertake any extra work in his rest time or holidays if by so doing he is depriving an out-of-work member of a chance to obtain employment."[40] In Ghana, the rule of the single employer has only one exception: that of a public relations consultant. The Swiss regulations are more liberal and allow journalists to earn up to 20 per cent of their income from non-journalistic activities. These can be in public relations, commercial publicity or as head of a press service. However, journalists may not exploit their journalistic status in exercising these activities. The guide-lines laid down by the German radio-television networks mentioned earlier specify that the secondary activities allowed to employees may be in the business world,

Structure of the profession

subject to approval by management. Authorisation is not required for certain types of occasional work, such as scientific work, conferences and participation in trade union, political or religious activities, but if the journalist is elected to a municipal or parliamentary office, management must be informed.

Notes

[1] The first to be passed was law No. 12908 of 1946.

[2] Law of 30 December 1963.

[3] Law of 29 March 1935, modified by the law of 4 July 1974.

[4] Adopted by the IFJ at the Nice Congress, September 1978.

[5] ILO: *International standard classification of occupations* (ISCO), Revised edition 1968 (Geneva, 4th impression, 1981), section 1-59.15.

[6] Law No. 12908 of 1946.

[7] Law of 20 December 1979.

[8] Royal Commission on the Press: *Final report* (London, HMSO, 1977), pp. 167-169.

[9] F. F. Lehni: *Economic and social conditions of freelance journalists* (Brussels, International Federation of Journalists, Apr. 1977; mimeographed).

[10] For example, the law on work at home of 29 October 1974, in the Federal Republic of Germany, which allows certain categories of independent workers to enter into collective contracts *(Bericht der Bundesregierung über die Lage von Presse und Rundfunk in der Bundesrepublik Deutschland (1978)*, printed paper 8/2264, p. 124). Also refer to the French Labour Code in which article L. 761-2 specifies: "Any agreement whereby a newspaper undertaking obtains the services of a professional journalist ... in return for remuneration shall be deemed to constitute a contract of employment. It shall be deemed to constitute such a contract irrespective of the form and rate of the remuneration and of how the parties style the agreement."

[11] "L'agence France-Presse", in *Notes et études documentaires* (Paris, La documentation française), Nos. 4336-4337, 23 Nov. 1976.

[12] ibid., p. 29.

[13] ibid., p. 50.

[14] ISCO, op. cit., section 1-59.20.

[15] Royal Commission on the Press, op. cit., p. 155.

[16] Central Youth Employment Executive: *Journalism*, Choice of Careers, No. 83 (London, HMSO, 5th edition, 1974), pp. 14-15. See also the model organigram for the editing of a London newspaper in Advisory, Conciliation and Arbitration Service (ACAS): *Industrial relations in the national newspaper industry* (London, HMSO, 1976), p. 302.

[17] ISCO, op. cit., section 1-59.25.

[18] Central Youth Employment Executive, op. cit., pp. 12-13.

[19] ISCO, op. cit., section 1-59.30.

[20] ibid., section 1-63.40.

[21] Central Youth Employment Executive, op. cit., p. 11.

[22] ISCO, op. cit., section 1-59.35.

[23] Central Youth Employment Executive, op. cit., p. 28.

[24] ACAS, op. cit., p. 159.

[25] *Massen-Medien in Österreich* (Vienna, Internationale Publikationen Gesellschaft, 1977).

[26] Centre d'études et de recherches sur les qualifications (CEREQ): *Les journalistes, Etude statistique et sociologique de la profession* (Paris, La documentation française, 1974), pp. 27 ff.

[27] L. Furhoff, L. Jönsson and L. Nilsson: *Communication policies in Sweden* (Paris, UNESCO Press, 1974), p. 72.

[28] See May Katzen: *Mass communication: Teaching and studies at universities* (Paris, UNESCO Press, 1975). This book presents a world-wide survey of universities which provide teaching in journalism and of institutes or schools of journalism. The following pages have drawn heavily on this book.

[29] *Feuillets du Centre de formation et de perfectionnement des journalistes* (Paris), Spring 1978, No. 61, pp. 10-11.

[30] See *Bericht der Bundesregierung über die Lage von Presse und Rundfunk in der Bundesrepublik Deutschland (1978)*, op. cit., p. 117.

[31] See "L'agence France-Presse", op. cit., p. 52.

[32] Dosu Oyelude: *The press in West Africa* (Brussels, International Federation of Journalists, 1974), p. 62.

[33] ibid., p. 94.

[34] See the 1977 judgement relative to daily newspaper journalists (article 16).

[35] See ACAS, op. cit., pp. 160-161; Royal Commission on the Press, op. cit., pp. 172-173 and Appendix G in *Final report. Appendices* (London, HMSO, 1977); Central Youth Employment Executive, op. cit., pp. 32-34.

[36] Lehni, op. cit., pp. 31-32.

[37] See F. F. Lehni: *The situation of IFJ member unions* (Brussels, International Federation of Journalists, Feb. 1976; mimeographed), pp. 26-27.

[38] An amendment of 1981 to the law of 1955 on journalists recognised as such those employed as journalists, full time or part time, in, or for, one or several press enterprises.

[39] Law No. 66-27 of 30 April 1966 (article 402).

[40] J. Stapleton: *Communication policies in Ireland* (Paris, UNESCO Press, 1974), pp. 51-52.

EMPLOYMENT IN THE PROFESSION 2

With the dramatic development of various means of communication, the profession of journalism has undergone a remarkable expansion. However, it is still difficult to assess, even approximately, the number of active journalists in the world. In order to give a rough idea of the total number of people employed in this profession, it seems useful to begin by looking at the steady growth of the printed press in society as a whole.

SOCIETY AND THE PRESS

The role of the press in society can first be measured in terms of circulation figures. *La Gazette*, produced by Théophraste Renaudot in the seventeenth century, initially a monthly and later a weekly, had an average print-run of only 1,200 copies.[1] It is fairly certain that the first daily newspapers to appear in England, France, Germany and the United States in the seventeenth and eighteenth centuries had only a modest circulation. Today, the major dailies are distributed in hundreds of thousands, if not millions, of copies. Some of them have dozens of pages in each edition. In 1977, there were more than 8,000 daily newspapers of a general information nature in the world.[2] These overall figures obviously reflect different kinds of national situations (see table 3). Certain countries have only one daily and others none at all. Conversely, some countries have hundreds of dailies: 320 in Brazil, 410 in the Federal Republic of Germany, 930 in India, 270 in Mexico, 440 in Turkey, 690 in the USSR and 1,830 in the United States. Without analysing the situation too deeply, it is safe to say that this diversity is due to such factors as the size of the population, political organisation and the level of economic and cultural development.

More significant perhaps are the circulation figures in relation to population. The world average in 1977 for daily newspapers was 136 copies per thousand inhabitants, but this figure is also misleading inasmuch as it hides disparities between developed and developing countries

Table 3. Number and circulation of daily newspapers and other periodicals by country

Country	General information newspapers					Non-daily newspapers					Other periodicals			
	Daily newspapers														
	Year	Number	Circulation				Year	Number	Circulation			Year	Number	Circulation	
			Total (thousands)	Per 1,000 population				Total (thousands)	Per 1,000 population				Total (thousands)	Per 1,000 population
Africa														
Algeria	1977	4	236	13		1977	3	107	6		1977	39	413.6	23
United Republic of Cameroon	1976	3	30	5		1975	17	.	.		1975	41	.	.
Congo	1977	1	.	.		1977	5	25*	17*		.	.	.	.
Egypt	1976	10	3 012	79		1974	19	1 338	37		1974	186	1 182.9	32
Ivory Coast	1976	3	63	13		1976	2[1]	65[1]	.		.	.	.	.
Kenya	1976	3	154	11		.	.	.	.		.	.	.	.
Libyan Arab Jamahiriya	1976	2	64	26		1976	5	111	45		.	.	.	.
Morocco	1976	10	190[2]	.		1975	31	.	.		1976	63	145	8
Nigeria	1976	19	527[3]	.		1974	25	460	8		1974	25	210	3
Senegal	1976	1	25	5		.	.	.	.		1974	37	.	.
Sudan	1976	4	26[4]	.		1977	2	30	2		1973	20	.	.
United Republic of Tanzania	1977[5]	2	133	8		.	.	.	.		.	.	.	.
Togo	1976	1	7	3		.	.	.	.		.	.	.	.
Tunisia	1976[5]	5	232[6]	.		1977	107	732	121		1977	104	870	144
Uganda	1976	2	35	3		.	.	.	.		.	.	.	.
Upper Volta	1976	1	1.5	0.2		1976	3[1]	5.2[1]	.		.	.	.	.
Zaire	1976	6	45[4]	.		1974	6	21	1		1974	43	61	3
Zambia	1976	2	101	20		.	.	.	.		1977	3	18	4
Zimbabwe	1976	2	78	12		.	.	.	.		.	.	.	.

Employment in the profession

The Americas											
Argentina	1976	142							1972	1 360	
Bolivia	1976	13							1972	18*	
Brazil	1977	318		26	1972	63			1977	1 632	
Canada	1977	122	2 682 [7]	45	1972	13*	3 068*	27*	1977	953	46 076	1979
Chile	1977 [5]	42	5 083	221	1977	959	11 955	514	1977			
Colombia	1976	42	5 150		1977	1 215			1975	1 034		
Costa Rica	1976	6	1 330 [8]		1975	28	125	5				
Cuba	1976	16	210	104		8						
Dominican Republic	1976	10	208		1978	101			1978	284		
Ecuador	1978	37	350	46	1971	12			1975	127		
El Salvador	1976	12	331 [9]		1975	18	32	5	1974	23	100	129
Guatemala	1976	9	214 [10]	63	1974	8	236.2	305				
Guyana	1976	2	50	20								
Haiti	1976	6	92									
Honduras	1976	8	140 [10]	49	1974	10	381	190	1977	1 964		
Jamaica	1977	3	101		1977	483						
Mexico	1976	268	3 944 [11]	51	1977	1	18	474	1976	2	27	614
Nicaragua	1976	6	113	79								
Panama	1976	6	136	39	1975	31	2 799	179	1975	595	90.7	202
Paraguay	1976	4	106		1977	7	15	33	1977	21		
Peru	1977	30	828	51	1974	2	167.2	156				
Suriname	1977	7	33	74								
Trinidad and Tobago	1976	3	144 [4]		1977	9 281			1977	9 732		
United States	1977	1829	62 159	287	1977	48			1977	335		
Uruguay	1977	26			1977	3	500	39				
Venezuela	1977	54	2 263	178								

35

Table 3. (continued)

Country	General information newspapers							Non-daily newspapers					Other periodicals			
	Daily newspapers															
	Year	Number	Circulation				Year	Number	Circulation			Year	Number	Circulation		
			Total (thousands)	Per 1,000 population					Total (thousands)	Per 1,000 population				Total (thousands)	Per 1,000 population
Asia															
Afghanistan	1977	17	77	4		1975	11	89	5		1977	25	61.7	3	
Bangladesh	1976	28	350 [13]	.		.	.	.	.		1975	6	118	4	
Burma	1976	7	329	11		.	.	.	.		.	.	.	.	
Hong Kong	1977	83	1 393 [13]	.		1977	38	.	.		1977	267	257.5 [15]	.	
India	1977	929	10 672 [16]	.		1977	4 908	7 962 [17]	.		1975	8 844	.	.	
Indonesia	1976	178	2 358 [18]	.		.	.	.	.		.	.	.	.	
Islamic Republic of Iran	1976	23	473 [19]	.		1974	51	95.6	3		1974	176	536	17	
Iraq	1976	7	202 [10]	.		1974	6	.	.		1974	179	1 102	102	
Israel	1976	24	801 [19]	.		1978	96	.	.		1978	583	.	.	
Japan	1977	177	62 221	546		.	.	.	.		1977	25 604	.	.	
Jordan [20]	1977	5	85	29		1977	4	30	10		1977	40	100	35	
Democratic Kampuchea	1976	17	.	.		.	.	.	.		.	.	.	.	
Republic of Korea	1977	44	7 169	197		1977	117	2 294	63		1976	1 146	.	.	
Democratic People's Republic of Korea	1976	11	1 000 [14]	.		.	.	.	.		.	.	.	.	
Kuwait	1977	7	180	159		1977	19	145	128		1976	49	171	151	
Lebanon	1976	33	281 [21]	.		1977	28	.	.		1975	847	.	.	
Malaysia	1976	37	1 834 [8]	.		1977	28	.	.		1975	847	.	.	
Nepal	1976	29	96 [22]	.		1976	52	.	.		1976	94	.	.	

Employment in the profession

Country	Year					Year				
Pakistan	1976	103		121			1972	103			60
Philippines	1976	17	965 [23]	84			1975	101	2 530		8
Saudi Arabia	1976	12	919 [24]	8	30	3	1974	20	67		
Singapore	1977	10	143 [12]	4	297.4	129	1977	1 521			104
Sri Lanka	1977	22	497	196			1977	465	1 459.6		
Syrian Arab Republic	1976	7	65 [10]	6			1975	35			
Thailand	1977	23		71			1975	986			
United Arab Emirates	1977	3	2	3	2	8	1977	8	25		106
Europe											
Austria	1977	31	2 529	132			1977	2 206			
Belgium	1977	27	2 369	2	30	3	1977	9 651			
Bulgaria	1977	12	2 083	36	949	108	1977	1 470	8 491		964
Cyprus	1976	13	72 [26]	21	137	212					
Czechoslovakia	1977	29	4 453	111	984.1	65	1977	921	21 758.5	1 448
Denmark	1977	49	1 840	2	163	32	1974	3 594			
Finland	1977	60	2 202	245			1975	2 113			
France	1977	96	10 863	694	15 451	291	1977	13 716	183 379	3 455
German Democratic Republic	1977	39	8 317	32	8 931	532	1977	1 162	20 524	1 224
Federal Republic of Germany	1977	412	25 968	49	2 139		1974 [25]	867	85 305	1 378
Greece	1977	112	423	745			1977	748			
Hungary	1977	27	2 585	86	5 820.4	547	1977	898	13 276	1 247
Iceland	1977	6	123	6			1975	302			
Ireland	1977	7	702	54	1 672.6	524	1977	159	1 677.8 [27]	
Italy	1977	72	5 491	122			1977	7 390			
Netherlands	1976	67	4 371 [28]	152	902.9	67					
Norway	1977	82	1 740	76	337	83	1975	3 855			
Poland	1977	44	8 331	38	1 971	57	1977	2 446	30 436	877

Table 3. (continued)

Country	General information newspapers					Non-daily newspapers					Other periodicals			
	Daily newspapers													
	Year	Number	Circulation Total (thousands)		Per 1,000 population	Year	Number	Circulation Total (thousands)		Per 1,000 population	Year	Number	Circulation Total (thousands)	Per 1,000 population
Portugal	1977	28	527		54	1975	307			.	1977	901	.	.
Romania	1977	34	3 711		171	1978	24	712.9	*	33 *	1974	553	7 524	358
Spain	1977	143	4 710		128	1977	24	1 013		28	1977	5 508	55 352	1 509
Sweden	1977	112	4 358		528	1977	69	512		62	1977	3 690	.	.
Switzerland	1977	91	2 622		414	1977	169	882.5		139	1977	1 463	31 696	5 010
Turkey	1977	493	.		.	1977	618	.		.				
United Kingdom	1977	.	22 900		410	1975	1 092	.		.	1975	5 221	.	.
Yugoslavia	1977	26	2 085		96	1977	2 512	13 470		619	1977	1 509	14 293	657
Oceania														
Australia	1977	60	4 365		310	1977	507	9 126	*	648 *	1976	3 585 [29]	.	.
Fiji	1976	2	38		66	1976	4	46		79				
New Zealand	1976	39	848 [30]		.	1976	111	.		.	1976	4 653	.	.
Soviet Union														
USSR	1977	686	102 462		396	1977	7 237	67 621		261	1977	4 772 [31]	.	.
Byelorussian SSR	1977	27	2 368		251	1977	159	2 379		252	1977	153 [32]	2 140	227

* Provisional or estimated figure.
. Figures not available.

[1] For non-daily newspapers in rural areas only. [2] For 7 dailies only. [3] For 8 dailies. [4] For 2 dailies. [5] The figures are for morning dailies only. [6] For 4 dailies. [7] For 117 dailies. [8] For 35 dailies. [9] For 5 dailies. [10] For 146 dailies. [11] For parish bulletins, school papers and company magazines. [12] For 6 dailies. [13] For 19 dailies. [14] For 1 daily. [15] For 252 periodicals. [16] For 603 dailies. [17] For 2 444 newspapers. [18] For 50 dailies. [19] For 20 dailies. [20] The figures refer only to the Right Bank. [21] For 15 dailies. [22] For 13 dailies. [23] For 21 dailies. [24] For 16 dailies. [25] Weekly journals only. [26] For 10 dailies. [27] For 152 periodicals. [28] For 56 dailies. [29] Excluding humorous periodicals, parish bulletins, school papers and company magazines. [30] For 37 dailies. [31] Excluding parish bulletins, school papers and company magazines. [32] Excluding company magazines.

Sources. UNESCO: *Statistical Yearbook 1980* (Paris, 1981); United Nations: *Statistical Yearbook* (New York, 1981).

Note. In this table, the description "general information newspapers" refers to all periodicals whose aim is to present reports on current events. They are considered as dailies if they appear at least four times weekly and as non-dailies when they appear three times per week or less frequently. Publications classified as "other periodicals" are those which deal with subjects of a very general interest or which publish studies and reports on specialised subjects such as the law, finance, commerce, medicine, fashion, sport, etc. (specialised newspapers, reviews, magazines, etc.).

Employment in the profession

Table 4. Number and circulation of daily newspapers by regions, groups and countries

Regions and groups	Number of daily newspapers	Estimated circulation	
		Total (millions)	Per 1,000 population
World total [1]	8 210	443	136
Africa	180	9	21
Americas	3 110	92	158
Asia [1]	2 380	107	72
Europe	1 740	127	264
Oceania	110	6	268
USSR	690	102	394
Africa (excluding the Arab States)	150	5	15
North America	1 950	67	281
Latin America	1 160	25	72
Asia (excluding the Arab States) [1]	2 300	106	73
Arab States	110	5	30
Developed countries	4 700	366	321
Developing countries [1]	3 510	77	36

[1] Excluding China, the Democratic People's Republic of Korea and Viet Nam.
Source. UNESCO: *Statistical Yearbook 1980* (Paris, 1981).

and, even more so, between the extremes in these two groups (see tables 3 and 4). By way of comparison, the number of copies of daily newspapers in Africa per thousand inhabitants is a mere dozen or so, whereas in Europe, North America and Japan, it is several hundreds.

Publications other than general information dailies are generally speaking numerous and have high circulations, although again there is considerable national variation. This is especially notable in such countries as Belgium (9,651 publications), France (13,716 and 3,455 copies per thousand inhabitants), India (8,844), Japan (25,604), Switzerland (1,463 and 5,010 copies per thousand inhabitants), the USSR (67,621) and the United States (9,732).

It is true that, in many of the developing countries, distribution is generally confined to the main population centres and penetrates only minimally into areas where illiteracy is high or transport services are limited. Subject to this important reservation, it can be said that the printed press is a widespread, if not a universal, feature of our times.

The spoken press — that is, news through radio and television — is truly omnipresent. There is hardly a family, even in the poorest countries and remotest spots, which does not possess a radio set, if only a modest one, and which cannot receive news bulletins. And, in this context, there is no need to stress the role of radio in mobilising the population in certain contemporary political developments.

Profession: Journalist

NUMBER OF JOURNALISTS

Only a few countries have a body responsible for registering journalists as such. Moreover, the definitions adopted do not necessarily correspond with those given in Chapter 1. Thus, the data provided in this study can have only an indicative value. Table 5 gives these data for 28 countries.

No conclusion can be drawn from this table but a few observations are perhaps in order.

First, the number of journalists is growing steadily. This fact emerges from the chronological data made available by some countries. The number went up by 30 per cent in Austria from 1972 to 1976; by 55 per cent in Denmark from 1969 to 1978; by 45 per cent in France from 1969 to 1978; by 24 per cent in the Federal Republic of Germany from 1970 to 1976; [3] by 28 per cent in Italy from 1973 to 1977; by 11 per cent in Japan from 1970 to 1975 (numbers tripled between 1950 and 1975); by 58 per cent in Malaysia from 1969 to 1978; by 28 per cent in New Zealand from 1971 to 1976; by 40 per cent in Poland from 1970 to 1979 (excluding radio and television); and by 15 per cent in Sweden from 1972 to 1976. Australia, where figures were more or less stable from 1970 to 1976, is an exception.

Quantitatively, journalists do not represent an important professional group. When their numbers are related to those of the total working population, the figure is almost negligible: 1.7 per thousand in New Zealand; 1.4 per thousand in Japan and Sweden; 1.3 per thousand in Denmark and Hong Kong; 1 per thousand in the United Kingdom; 0.9 per thousand in the Federal Republic of Germany; 0.6 per thousand in France and the United States; 0.5 per thousand in Austria; 0.4 per thousand in Australia, Belgium and Ireland; 0.3 per thousand in Italy and Pakistan; 0.2 per thousand in Honduras; and less than 0.1 per thousand in the United Republic of Cameroon and India. If these figures are compared with the numbers for professional, technical and related workers (the 0/1 group in the *International standard classification of occupations*), of which journalists are a part, the figures are 24 per thousand in Hong Kong; 19 per thousand in Japan; 12 per thousand in New Zealand; 11 per thousand in Pakistan; 6 per thousand in Sweden; 4.6 per thousand in Honduras; 4 per thousand in France and the United States; 3.4 per thousand in the United Republic of Cameroon; 3.3 per thousand in Italy; and 2.1 per thousand in India.

It is pointless to make international comparisons on the basis of these figures in view of their obvious inadequacy. However, given the considerable role played by the press, these figures are a striking example, as occurs so frequently, of the disproportion between the number of workers in certain categories and the role of those workers in modern society.

Employment in the profession

A priori, there is no reason why women should not practise the profession of journalism and, in fact, there would seem to be an increasing number of women who write articles or — in certain countries, at least — present the news on radio or television. However, in the few countries for which relevant statistical data are available, women are still only a minority in the world of journalism. In France in 1978, there were 3,422 women journalists out of a total of 15,563 (22 per cent); in the Federal Republic of Germany in 1976, there were 11,000 out of a total of 36,000 (31 per cent); [4] there were 9,100 out of 74,100 in Japan in 1975 (12 per cent); and there were 387 out of 1,736 in New Zealand in 1971 (22 per cent). A British study [5] estimated this minority to be one-eighth in the United Kingdom in 1974 for newspapers but, according to the same study, there were relatively more women working on magazines and periodicals than on newspapers, because many of those publications were aimed at a female readership. According to another study,[6] 35 per cent of new recruits to the press in 1975 were women as against 25 per cent in 1966, which would seem to suggest that the low minority noted in 1974 has since gone up. In the United States in 1970, more than 35 per cent of reporters were women.[7] The International Organisation of Journalists calculated that 25 per cent of journalists in Czechoslovakia in 1976 were women as compared with 3 per cent 50 years earlier.[8] In Poland, the proportion is 35 per cent.[9]

The conditions of work in the profession, such as irregular and late working hours, could certainly account for the exclusion of women with family responsibilities. On closer examination, however, it can be noted that certain special areas of the press (depending on the subjects handled and the target audience) have more attraction for women journalists. This is the case, as has just been observed, with the sections of the press aimed at women in the United Kingdom. The situation is similar in France [10] where in 1974 women represented 69 per cent of the editorial staff in the women's press, 50 per cent in the children's press, 57 per cent in publications dealing with practical matters of daily life, 43 per cent in the press for young people and 47 per cent in the press aimed at adolescents. In the same country, moreover, there appeared to be a concentration of women in certain types of employment: in the period from 1964 to 1971, women represented 88 per cent of the stenographers, 45 per cent of the translators and 23 per cent of the make-up staff, whereas they represented only 10 per cent of the editors, 7 per cent of the foreign correspondents, 6 per cent of the star reporters and 1 per cent of the press photographers. A note issued in April 1982 by the Ministry for Women's Rights confirmed this situation by pointing out that women are in the minority in television jobs and for the most part are confined to the background, while men enjoy the spotlight on the television screen, that the star reporters and announcers are predominantly men and that, out of 961 journalists, only 115 are women. These figures illustrate clearly

Profession: Journalist

Table 5. Numbers of journalists in selected countries

Country	1969	1970	1971	1972	1973	1974	1975	1976	1977	1978
Australia [1]		2 442				2 403	2 299	2 392		
Austria				1 246				1 624		
Belgium						1 600*				
United Republic of Cameroon [2]										230*
Costa Rica	109									251
Denmark [3]	2 224	2 342	2 453	2 596	2 733	2 854	2 992	3 136	3 318	3 456
Ethiopia										400*
Finland										6 000 [4]
France	10 754	11 943	12 429	12 558	13 018	13 349	13 635	14 236	14 673	15 563
Federal Republic of Germany [5]		29 000						36 000*		24 059
Guyana										100*
Honduras										143*
Hong Kong [6]								2 530*		
Hungary						3 250				
India	10 000*[7]									
Iraq	334 [8]									
Ireland										2 600
Italy [9]					4 748	5 446	5 739	6 151	6 057	470
Japan		66 565					74 000			
Libyan Arab Jamahiriya							176	182	173	
Malaysia [10]	147	144	151	171	187	180	183	231	230	250
New Zealand [11]			1 736					2 224		
Pakistan										7 000*
Poland								5 865		5 200 [12]
Sweden [13]				5 083						

42

Employment in the profession

Switzerland	3 150 *
United Kingdom	26 000 *
United States [14]	39 000 *

* Estimated.
. Figures not available.

[1] Members of the Australian Journalists' Association employed by the daily newspapers which are affected by the judgement concerning daily newspapers in state capitals. [2] Public sector only. [3] Active members (the number of persons in the private press is said to be "insignificant"). [4] 1980. [5] For 1970 and 1976, the figure refers to members of the Danish Union of Journalists. [6] For 142 press organs and five radio and television stations. [7] 1967. [8] 1968. [9] Excluding stringers. [10] New Straits Times Press (Malaysia) Berhad. Nanyang Press (Malaya) Sdn. Berhad progressed from 114 in 1969 to 152 in 1978. [11] Journalists, reporters, editors, sub-editors. [12] 1979. [13] Members of the Swedish Union of Journalists. [14] Reporters only. "publicists" (including writers, lecturers, etc., in addition to journalists); for 1978, journalists

enough the problems women face, in journalism as elsewhere, in breaking down the barriers of a deeply entrenched socio-cultural society. It will be seen later on that women journalists, once they have embarked on their career, do not always enjoy equal opportunity — or anything like it — with their masculine colleagues.

Notes

[1] On the origins of the printed press, see for example J. M. Auby and R. Ducos-Ader: *Droits de l'information* (Paris, Dalloz, 1976), pp. 21 ff.

[2] UNESCO: *Statistical Yearbook 1980* (Paris, 1981).

[3] Based on official statistics for "publicists" (including writers, lecturers, etc., in addition to journalists).

[4] ibid.

[5] Central Youth Employment Executive, op. cit., p. 37.

[6] Royal Commission on the Press, op. cit., p. 179.

[7] United States Department of Labor, Bureau of Labor Statistics: "Employment outlook for writing occupations", in *Occupational Outlook Handbook*, 1972-73 edition.

[8] Radi Vassilev: *La condition sociale des journalistes: Enquête comparative internationale-I* (Budapest, Interpress, 1976), p. 161.

[9] Tadeusz Kupis: "The education and further qualifications of Polish journalists", in *Democratic Journalist* (Prague), No. 4/79.

[10] See CEREQ, op. cit., pp. 61-69.

TECHNOLOGICAL AND ECONOMIC CONSTRAINTS AND EMPLOYMENT PROBLEMS

3

The press and audio-visual media — the main employers of journalists — are in the throes of profound technological and economic changes which are today affecting many aspects of the lives of journalists. This study does not purport to cover the whole field of communications, and the following pages are thus mainly devoted to the press. However, the grave problems faced by journalists on account of the extension of television, and particularly cable television, should not be overlooked.

TECHNOLOGICAL EVOLUTION

"Light has put an end to lead": this expression is a good illustration of the way press printing processes have been transformed over the last 12 years or so.[1] How exactly have they changed?

In the traditional process, the basic instrument for composition is the linotype machine. By tapping the keys, the linotype operator releases small metal plates — matrices — from a magazine in which they are lined up one behind the other. Each matrix is inset with the shape of a letter for reproduction. They are then dropped into a composing stick and transferred, line by line, to the type foundry. Molten lead is poured into the matrices and, after cooling, a line of characters in relief is formed.

The following stage is page make-up. The lines of lead type, and illustrations reproduced in relief on zinc plates (i.e. by photogravure), are arranged in a large steel frame, or chase, in accordance with the instructions of the editorial staff. A flexible cardboard sheet, the flong, is placed on the frame and receives, under pressure, an impression of the pages in negative. The flong is placed in a semi-cylindrical cradle, molten lead is poured in and a half-cylinder carrying the page in relief, a stereotype, is produced. Finally the stereotype, which is ready for printing, is placed on the rotary press.

But it is earlier in the process than this that the most revolutionary changes have taken place. After the Second World War, a system was introduced which made it possible to reproduce identical pages for several newspapers in different cities: this took the form of a perforated tape which incorporated the elements needed for line division and word-breaks and operated the linotype machine by means of a tape reader. Later, the production of the tape, until then handled by a linotype operator, was transferred to computers: the tape is continuously perforated without the operator having to worry about justification or word-breaks at the end of a line and the computer, according to its programme, reproduces the checked tape with all the markings required for the linotype operation. This was itself a considerable advance which, combined with other improvements in the machine, led to very fast composing speeds and meant that composing rooms could be remotely controlled.

But the real revolution was the advent of photocomposition, which is based on the principle of the photography of characters, or more exactly of composed text, for printing and the transfer of the characters, or text, to film or paper.

In simple language, the operations can be described as follows: texts are keyed directly into a cathode ray tube terminal (CRT) which is linked to the computer; the operator types the text (which then appears on the screen), makes any corrections required and stores it — often in a central memory which can be some distance away. The text can be recalled at any time for consultation, verification or modification. At a given moment, a built-in photographic device reproduces the final text on the basis of the programmed presentation (typographical characters, justification, paragraphing, etc.). Once the photocomposition is completed, the film or paper is finally made up on squared paper which serves as a gauge.

Using the photogravure process, a plate in relief can be printed off the prototype page, which then gives the mould and the stereotype in the traditional way. However, it is the offset process which is now becoming more and more dominant, a process which involves making the photographic transfer of prototypes on to thin, flexible plates which, without any other operation, are placed on the rotary cylinders. Lead type no longer plays any role. Photography has banished it completely.

In a still more advanced stage, the photocomposition device can, on the instructions of the computer, produce not just the page elements still to be pasted up, but a film of the whole page, ready for printing. Thus, the process of "electronic editing" is complete.

New processes and new tools have inevitably had their effect on the jobs performed by press technicians. Those most affected are the compositors and typesetters. The linotype operator has given way to the keyboard operator — that is, those responsible for typing texts on CRTs. Proof-readers and technicians involved in page make-up and plate-

Technological and economic constraints

making are fewer in number and their jobs are subject to many changes. A more detailed account of the upheavals that this group of workers has undergone because of various technological changes is outside the scope of this study. However, while not of vital importance, the consequences of these new methods on the work of journalists are worth mentioning.

The job security of journalists is not directly or seriously threatened. Journalists are still needed for finding and writing stories, preparing them for publication, laying them out, etc. However, the investment required to transform the composing rooms might accelerate the tendency towards concentration mentioned in the next section and, if so, editorial teams might be in danger of being dispensed with or of being fundamentally reorganised. Conversely, there are now photocomposition devices and small rotary presses which are simpler in operation and which take up less space. These might encourage the appearance of new newspapers requiring only a modest investment. But the problem of organising the distribution of such publications with a minimum budget will still remain.

The threat to the employment of journalists could come from other directions, although the reality and dimensions of the threat are difficult to evaluate at the moment. For example, news agencies no longer confine themselves to supplying short, concise news reports; they now offer complete stories which can be bought by newspapers as a package. On the technical level — and this process is already current — nothing prevents newspapers from being partly made up of pages completely edited and composed by news agencies and transmitted on coded tapes to the newspaper's printing room, or directly from one computer to another. The result is that the editorial team on the newspaper is bypassed. In addition, in an increasing number of countries telematics or cable television enable all kinds of practical information to be received at home on television screens, a service which was formerly the exclusive domain of local newspapers. How many potential readers are being lost and will be lost by these newspapers as a result? Even the survival of the newspaper itself could be threatened!

For the moment, however, it is not so much the job security of journalists which is affected by the new technology as the nature of their work. In this context, there is one immediate observation to be made: the demarcation line between the sphere of influence of the printer and that of the journalist is blurred in various ways. Certainly the territory between the computer output and the rotary printers remains in the hands of the printing technicians, even though considerably modified. But before this stage of the process is reached, the situation is far less clear.[2]

At the text composition stage, much depends on whether the textual presentation is complicated, with graphics for example, or whether it is straightforward. The more complicated the text, the more the technical sector dominates as opposed to the editorial side. For simple texts, it is enough for the typist to know how to use certain special keyboard signs, such as that indicating the end of a paragraph. In such cases, would it be illogical to expect reporters to type their stories themselves at the terminal? The main changes for them would be that their typewriters would be linked to the computer and that they would be obliged to perfect their typewriting skills.

It might be assumed that the graphic layout (choice of type size, weight of type-face, headlines, etc.) should be the responsibility of the technician rather than the journalist, but in past practice decisions at this level have always been taken by a member of the editorial staff. Should a member of the editorial staff and the technician sit in front of the CRT screen together, the former for decisions and the latter for their execution? Or should the former, once trained in the use of codes, replace the latter?

The problems of making up the pages raise similar questions. The most advanced devices which can display several columns on the screen simultaneously are complicated to handle and would seem to require the skills of a technician. But, here again, the decisions on the positioning of articles and illustrations should be handled by a member of the editorial staff. Are two people required for this work?

These are important questions. Naturally, the newspaper management is out to reduce production costs and staffing represents a high percentage of these costs.[3] But that is only one aspect of the question. The switchover to new equipment and production methods is a delicate undertaking. For staff to adapt themselves to these new requirements is even more delicate in view of the many types of human problems caused by these changes: the creation of new functions and the abolition of old ones, the transfer of responsibilities, the modification of tasks, the acquisition of new qualifications, the elimination of jobs, the conflict of interests between various professional categories, etc.

Yet the new trend has arrived, and in a big way. The technological revolution started in the United States press at the end of the sixties and was quick to assert itself. In 1970, there were still 10,290 linotype machines in service in that country, but in 1974 there were only 3,892 and now they are no longer produced in the United States. In the same period, the number of CRTs used by the press went from 23 to 1,666 and the number of typewriters for optical character reading more than doubled from 1973 to 1974.[4] Most newspapers in other developed countries and in some of the developing ones have followed suit, often with some hesitation. According to one estimate, stated by its author to be only approximate, the penetration rate in 1981 of the new technology was 100 per cent in the United States and Canada, 90 per cent in Finland, 80 per cent in Japan, 60 per cent in most parts of Europe, 15 per cent in India and near to zero per cent in most of the countries on the African continent.[5]

Technological and economic constraints

The news agencies have not been slow to adopt the new computer techniques. For them the problem is not to shorten the chain which links editorial to printing but to reduce the time between receipt of the information and dispatch of the processed news. The computer, with its accessory the display unit where the news takes shape and is made up by the editor, has supplied the answer.[6] The agency has derived the benefit: reception and processing of dispatches, consultation of archives and management of the company can be integrated into a single system. Clients also benefit since they receive more voluminous, more reliable information more rapidly, and even faster if their computer is linked to that of the agency. A striking example is the service supplied by Reuters in New York to one of the local cable television companies: Reuters's computer sends information via coaxial cable at a speed of 70,000 words a second; at the other end, the client's computer extracts and displays from this stream of data that information which it has been programmed to select: stock exchange prices, racing results, etc.[7]

In this sector, perhaps more than on newspapers, journalists find themselves working in new conditions: in the automated news agency, reporters are now riveted to their keyboards and screens; in addition to sifting the news and rewriting dispatches, they now have to learn how to handle techniques previously alien to the profession.

Two other technological innovations which have had an impact on the employment or the jobs of journalists should be mentioned. Since September 1980, the *International Herald Tribune* has been distributed simultaneously in Europe and Asia, thanks to satellite transmission between Paris and Hong Kong (at five minutes per page); this obviously threatens the employment of certain members of the editorial staff. At another level, a new device — a case containing a typewriter equipped with a transmitter — enables reporters in the field to transmit the typewritten version of their articles directly to their newspaper's computer by simply plugging in on a telephone line: this is "telecomposition", a development which is bound to have an effect on the working methods of journalists on outside assignments.

Journalists and their unions have naturally looked for ways to protect their professional interests from the threat of these technological innovations.

At the Fourteenth World Congress, held in Nice in 1978, the International Federation of Journalists defined its position on the new technology as follows: [8]

1. The new technology should enable the journalist to enhance his creativity and improve his working conditions and material rewards.
2. Journalists should participate in all stages of planning and introducing of new techniques.
3. The new techniques should not impose on the journalist tasks which may interfere with his creativity.

4. The introduction of new techniques should not result in the loss of jobs for those presently employed.
5. On the introduction of new technology into a particular paper, any journalist there who prefers to continue using traditional methods should be free to do so without prejudice to his present employment.
6. The IFJ recommends its affiliated unions of journalists to co-operate with the graphical unions.
7. No new technique should be introduced until there has been full discussion, negotiation and agreement between management and unions.
8. All workers operating the new techniques should be under constant health control, independent of the employers, either at the place of work or outside, and at the choice of the workers concerned. There should be more research into the effects, physical and psychological, of the new techniques.
9. All training and retraining arising out of new techniques should be done within working hours and at the management's expense.
10. Journalists and their unions should insist that no copy can be published without being handled by the editorial staff.
11. Each journalist should have a hard copy of matter he has produced on the screen. Hard copy of all material reaching the screen should be available whether it comes from a news agency or any outside source ...

Moreover, the International Federation of Journalists, together with the International Graphical Federation, drew up a joint statement on this subject (Copenhagen, 21 January 1980).[9] The two organisations reaffirmed the need to preserve the traditional division of work between editorial and production departments. They proclaimed the right of workers to participate in decisions on the application of new technology and requested that all staff be given appropriate training. They insisted on measures for health protection and opposed all salary reductions or any professional downgrading which might result from the application of these techniques. They asked that the increase in productivity be compensated by a reduction in working hours (35-hour week, educational leave, shorter professional life).

The various elements are for the most part contained in the statement of claims by national trade unions and some of them have already been incorporated in collective agreements between publishers on the one side, and print workers and journalists on the other, jointly or separately.

Under the terms of a collective agreement concluded on 20 March 1978 for the whole of the Federal Republic of Germany,[10] reporters cannot be compelled to work on the display terminals except for the keying in of their story, and then only if they would have typed it themselves anyway. Printing technicians are granted priority of employment in electronic composition jobs for eight years following the introduction of the new technology, with maintenance of their former wage until the age of retirement. Other clauses concern the limitation of hours of work on the display screens, the possible retraining of employees and conditions of dismissal.

Technological and economic constraints

In Austria, based on an agreement of 11 May 1981 between representatives of journalists, print workers and the employers' organisations for graphic industries and newspapers, the introduction of integrated systems of word-processing in the composition of dailies and weeklies is recognised as indispensable, but is subject to a number of conditions.[11] Some of these conditions are of particular interest to journalists. For example, editors will check all stories before they are passed to the technical processing section. The professional worth of journalists will not be assessed on the basis of competence at the VDU (Visual Display Unit). Normally, they will use the screen only to revise, correct or modify their texts. They cannot be obliged to make the first version unless they are in the habit of typing their articles and, in that case, it is their responsibility to include typographical instructions. Finally, journalists have the right to refuse to work on the VDU for eight years after adoption of the system — and even up to their retirement for those of 50 years of age and over with five years of service — without adverse effects on their employment. It should also be noted that management advisory boards are to be consulted as far as possible in advance, and that information and publicity agencies and outside newspapers may not directly introduce data into the integrated system for five years after its adoption.

At the end of 1981, the General Association of Professional Journalists in Belgium reached an agreement with the publishers of daily newspapers on the same subject.[12] The main points of this agreement prohibited any dismissals arising from the adoption of new techniques; confined journalists to editorial tasks; guaranteed their freedom of expression and creativity; and involved them in any plans to introduce new systems likely to affect the organisation of the editorial department.

In Canada, certain company agreements (for example, Pacific Press Ltd., Montreal Star Ltd.) oblige employers to give staff ample notice of their intention to adopt new methods or new equipment; not to make any of their permanent employees redundant because of modernisation; to provide a comparable job without loss of salary for any surplus staff; and to guarantee them the necessary retraining.

A detailed agreement was also signed in Denmark on 18 January 1977 between the Association of Journalists and the Association of Newspaper Publishers. It provides for the setting up of a special local joint committee before the installation of any equipment likely to have direct or indirect consequences on the working conditions of journalists. This committee is to be consulted on matters of salary, dismissal, renewal of contracts, professional training and working hours. Graphic screens for page make-up can be used only by typographers, who are responsible for all corrections not directly linked to the original creation. Terminals set up in the news-rooms must be used for the original work at all journalistic stages from writing to page make-up; editorial staff must be able to receive copies of the text which they have keyed into the terminal, for example, by means of a print-out.

The Collective Bargaining Program adopted by the Newspaper Guild in the United States calls on local unions to agree with employers that no speed or precision criteria will be set up for using the new equipment and that skills in handling this equipment will not be a criterion for the allocation of work. The agreement concluded between the Newspaper Guild and the two major news agencies — Associated Press (AP) and United Press International (UPI) — stipulates that advance notice (three months for AP and four for UPI) must be given to the union before the introduction of any equipment likely to cause a reduction of staff, and that any reduction must be achieved through natural wastage.

In Finland, the journalists' union and the printers' trade union adopted a common attitude in 1976, stating that they were in favour of the new technology, provided that no employee was adversely affected. In the following year, they reached an agreement with the employers: all newspaper publishers must conclude a local agreement on the introduction of technical innovations. This agreement, which must be approved by the unions and the employers' associations, will specify the types of equipment and methods of introduction, as well as the projected investment; in particular, it will contain an individual guarantee of employment for each member of the staff, it being understood that all eventual staff reductions will be the result of natural wastage.[13]

An agreement was reached in 1976 at Agence France-Presse whereby any journalist considered unable to work on the VDU would be given another post; editorial responsibilities would be specified; the time allowed for the correction of copy would be determined, etc. Another agreement in 1977 provided for the fixing of a special bonus, the amount being subject to adjustment in certain circumstances, such as work on the terminal; the question of staffing would be examined step by step as computerisation was installed at the news desk; the daily working shift at news desks was fixed at seven hours, with breaks taken on a rotating basis and not exceeding 60 minutes. In March 1978, several French unions for journalists and graphic workers agreed on common action in the face of new composition and printing techniques. Among other points, the agreement stipulated that the introduction of these techniques must not result in unemployment or disqualification; that advance information must be supplied to the various categories of staff involved; that there must be discussions with them; and that no separate agreement likely to damage the interests of one or the other category should be allowed. It was also agreed that the text input must go back to the graphic workers and that the system adopted for text layout must guarantee editorial staff their normal rights. In short, the responsibility for the idea remains with the journalist up to the proof-reading stage and the responsibility for technical production remains with the graphic workers. However, no negotiations have as yet been opened with the federations of press employers on these matters.

In Greece, in 1980, a conflict between publishers and typographers was ended through the mediation of a journalists' union. It was agreed to set up a commission, composed of publishers, journalists and typographers, responsible for examining the conditions for application of the new technology.[14] The work of the commission resulted in proposals which served as a basis for a law adopted in 1981, designed to find a solution to loss of employment caused by the adoption of the new technology. In practice, this law protects mainly the typographers.

In Italy, a national collective agreement was signed by the Italian Federation of Newspaper Publishers (FIEG) and the National Federation of the Italian Press (FNSI) on 29 June 1977. It contained a number of general principles on the new technology. The contracting parties committed themselves to an examination of all aspects of programmes of technical modernisation every six months; at company level this examination was to be carried out whenever circumstances made it necessary. On the introduction of the new procedures, the professional autonomy of journalists, the collective character of intellectual work and the organisational system of the work of journalists, based on the sharing of assignments and the allocation of responsibilities, had to be respected. Any surplus of reporters would be reabsorbed through the elimination of overtime and normal staff wastage.

A few months later, on 29 April 1978, the same federation of journalists (FNSI) and the United Federation of Printing Workers (FULPC) decided on the creation of a permanent national joint committee which, along with the periodic examinations of the FIEG mentioned above, would be responsible for co-ordinating the installation of the new technology throughout the country; and of joint committees in each press enterprise, made up of representatives from the production council and the editorial committee, which would be empowered to supervise the entire cycle of production of the newspaper.

In Norway, the Trade Union for Graphic Artists put in a plea to have a clause added to its own collective agreement in order to obtain from the labour tribunal in 1978 recognition of its exclusive right to use the VDUs in all sections of the newspaper where these machines operated. However, the judges stated that the strict application of this clause was not compatible with systems required by the new technology and invited the graphic artists' union and the journalists' union to negotiate practical solutions.[15]

In the United Kingdom, the National Union of Journalists (NUJ) has certainly instructed its members not to use direct production terminals without the agreement of the printers' union, but prolonged conflicts with several large newspapers have so far not been resolved satisfactorily for the three partners involved: newspaper management, journalists and printing staff.[16]

In Sweden, an agreement was reached in 1978 between the graphic arts trade unions and the journalists' unions under which the jobs arising from the new technology would be shared between graphic arts workers and journalists before the beginning of negotiations with employers.[17] The two unions agreed, at the beginning of 1980, to respect each other's domain and to present a common front to employers. The agreement, which was subsequently signed with the press employers' organisation in May of the same year, guaranteed that the installation of the new technology would be carried out without any redundancies and that the retraining of journalists, print workers and other employees would take place during working hours. Each category was to retain its area of competence. However, professional demarcation would be less rigid than in the past: for example, journalists would be able to put 30 per cent of their copy on the terminal themselves.[18]

The agreement signed on 1 January 1979 between the Swiss Federation of Journalists and the Swiss Association of Newspaper Publishers contains firm guarantees to editorial staff.[19] It stipulates that "editorial staff must be informed and consulted at the start of any plans or work on installing such systems". Unless the regular use of electronics is intrinsic to a specific job, "the journalist himself decides whether it is technically advisable to use electronic news-gathering equipment to do his job". This agreement was followed by another on 4 April of the same year between the same two partners, this time including the Newspaper Union of French-speaking Switzerland.[20] The same principles apply. The agreement states, for example, that "the journalist cannot be limited to working on an electronic console" and that "the system must be designed to allow journalists to make any necessary text changes before publication, and to obtain print-out of the copy fed into the computer memory" (for proof-reading, etc.). It is also stipulated that the publisher cannot cancel a journalist's contract when the newspaper is computerised unless it is impossible for equivalent and acceptable employment to be found. If the journalist is made redundant, "mobility compensation" must be paid for one year, to make up for any possible loss of salary. In addition, all journalists required to use electronic equipment will receive suitable training during working hours. Eye examinations will be carried out during the first weeks of work on the visual screen, and yearly thereafter.

As can be seen from these examples, the introduction of new technology has not been taken lightly by the journalists' unions. Refusal to accept it has become the exception. But there are still certain lines of resistance which go from a clear demand for guaranteed employment and pay to the stubborn defence of traditional rights and freedom to choose the equipment in certain conditions. Compared with the problems created in other sectors through technological innovation, the situation is complicated by the fact that it involves not only newspaper management and journalists, but also the interests of a third party, namely, the print workers, probably on an even more fundamental level. This is why journalists and production staff are increasingly concerned to reach a common understanding. It is also evident that the situation varies considerably from one country or one press enterprise to another, depending on the forces at play between the interested parties.

ECONOMIC CONSTRAINTS

Like any other enterprise, a press organisation does not live in an economic vacuum. It is subject to variations in the business climate. This is partly because its product is not absolutely indispensable: when private individuals have to cut down their spending, among the first items to be cut out are newspapers. In addition, financial problems oblige companies to trim their advertising budgets, at least temporarily. Advertising revenue for a newspaper is equal to, if not more than, sales revenue [21] and a prolonged drop in advertising revenue can be a mortal blow for newspapers, already badly hit by competition from radio and television.

Other economic difficulties are of a structural nature. The advent of audio-visual information has obviously dealt a blow to the daily printed press. Although the complementary nature of the three great information media cannot be denied (radio announces, television presents visually, the newspapers explain), it is still a fact that radio and television affect the press adversely in three ways: first, as has been noted, in depriving the press of part of its advertising revenue; second, in reducing the time spent in reading, which affects both newspapers and books; and finally, in countries where a licence fee is charged on radio and television sets, by absorbing a part of the resources devoted to leisure and information.[22]

At the same time, the different elements that determine the sales price of a newspaper have gone up considerably, in particular, the price of newsprint and ink, the amortisation of equipment and the salaries of journalists and printers. The sales price has not always followed the same upward spiral, either because it has been government policy to keep it low or because price increases have been spontaneously limited by the strictures of the market (that is, stagnation or drop in circulation).

These various factors have placed many newspaper companies in a delicate situation. Some have simply disappeared. Others have found their salvation, or an even stronger base, by combining with other newspaper companies or by joint production agreements, in whole or in part: editorial teams, printing, advertising management, distribution networks, etc.

This explains the increasing tendency towards press mergers, principally caused by economic and technical factors. According to a report by the Council of Europe, the number of independent production units — that is, those operating separately and equipped with all the required facilities — dropped by about 35 per cent between 1955 and 1973 in the European countries. In Austria, there were 34 production units for dailies in 1950 and only 19 in 1975.[23] In France, the number of independent units in the provincial press fell from 107 in 1951 to 42 in 1973.[24] In the Federal Republic of Germany, there were 540 dailies with 16.4 million copies sold in 1962 and 459 dailies with 20.6 million copies sold in 1972; the number of complete editorial teams was 225 in 1954 for all newspapers and periodicals, dropping to 190 in 1963 and 130 in 1973; press monopoly extends to nearly a third of the cities and provinces.[25] In Italy, there were 110 units in 1966 and 84 in 1969.[26] In 1967, there were 40 independent companies producing 56 publications in the Netherlands and, by 1976, only 28 for 49 publications.[27] The number of dailies in Sweden dropped from 216 in 1945 to 149 in 1970, whereas the total circulation rose from 2.9 million to 4.6 million copies. Of 120 Swiss dailies, only 85 have a full editorial staff. In the United Kingdom in 1976, two publishers between them controlled more than 65 per cent of the national daily "popular press" and two others 76 per cent of the national daily "quality newspapers".[28]

In the United States, between 1880 and 1968, the number of cities with two or more dailies in competition fell from 239 to 45; the journalists' union — the Newspaper Guild — made an appeal to Congress in 1979 to adopt a law fixing a ceiling for the number of newspapers or the size of circulation that a single group could control.[29] In Japan, of the 172 dailies produced in 1976, the "three big ones" alone — a further sign of concentration — had a circulation of about 30 million copies, more than 50 per cent of total circulation.[30]

The Australian press is also characterised by strong concentration and much overlapping of interests. Each of the main groups controls several newspapers in the same state and extends its interests to other states. One newspaper in Victoria belongs jointly to two dailies of this state, but one of the two, in turn, is controlled by a daily in New South Wales. A company with headquarters in South Australia has interests in newspapers in New South Wales, Victoria and in the Northern Territory, and publishes newspapers in Queensland and Western Australia. Several have holdings in radio and television.

Company mergers and the various systems of co-operation between newspapers are not the only signs of the structural changes which have modified the economic climate of the press in recent decades. To these can be added the buying of shares and the acquisition of capital interests outside the world of the press. Thus, the shares of a newspaper can be part of a portfolio which otherwise, if not mainly, is essentially composed

Technological and economic constraints

of industrial and commercial holdings. Sometimes newspaper shares change hands for reasons which have no bearing on the concept of news or the desire to influence public opinion, but rather are related to the movement of capital.

Journalists thus run the risk of becoming objects of transaction, in the same way as furniture and real estate. When the ownership changes, the newspaper's policy can change; the holders of posts can also change through decisions of the new management or resignation of former occupants who are unwilling to accept the new policy line. Regrouping of editorial staffs can lead to the elimination of certain posts. In the press, as in all other forms of activity, economic concentration often threatens employment.

It is for this reason, but also partly to ensure pluralism in the information sector, that governments come to the aid of the press. In certain countries, the State does not interfere at all; this is the case, for example, in Australia, Japan, New Zealand, Pakistan and the United Kingdom. But in other countries — leaving aside the extreme case where the State directly owns the organs of the press and where the question of pluralism of information is therefore academic — extensive aid is given by the public authorities.

In France, it takes two forms. Direct aid, written into the state budget (461 million francs in 1978), includes subscriptions by the State to Agence France-Presse, reimbursement to the Post Office for reduced telephone communication rates, a subsidy for the purchase of printing materials, a subsidy for railway transport, aid to the French press overseas and reimbursement of the value added tax. There is also indirect aid, resulting from loss of revenue by the Treasury or by local communities (more than 2,000 million francs in 1978): exoneration from certain taxes, the right to deduct projected investments from taxable profits, preferential postal charges and special rates for press cables and the renting of specialised cable connections. To this can be added exceptional subsidies, for example to dailies with low circulations or limited advertising revenue. The total of this aid has been estimated at 20 per cent of the total gross amount of sales.[31] It is obvious that these various forms of aid keep the price per copy at a low level.

In Sweden, the support given to the press by the State is also considerable. A credit fund was set up in 1969 granting loans on generous terms, initially for investment. Since 1970 there has been a distribution service at reduced rates. A production subsidy has been paid since 1971 to newspapers with small circulations; it is in proportion to the amount of space taken up by the editorial pages and is aimed at compensating for low advertising revenue. Since 1976, subsidies for development have been granted to newspapers with large circulations but in temporary financial difficulty. A system of co-operation subsidies aimed at encouraging the joint adoption of technological methods was set up in the same year. In the fiscal year 1978/79, state subsidies amounted to 285 million Swedish crowns for the daily press and 48 million for the journals of representative associations. The aid package also includes preferential postal rates, exemption from value added tax and a concessionary rate of tax on advertising. In the view of the Government the contraction in the press sector has been halted by these measures and the more or less general adoption of the new technology has been facilitated through the availability of credit funds.

The above provides two examples of countries where public authorities have granted generous aid in many different ways. Elsewhere, this aid is more limited. The most common form of support is:

— direct subsidies: in Belgium, in the United Republic of Cameroon (where, according to the Government, "the State is virtually the only promoter of the press"), in the Congo (where, again according to the Government, "all press organs, in one form or another, are paid for out of the state budget"), in Ireland and Spain (for the modernisation of equipment), in Italy (by way of aid to small enterprises or for the renewal of equipment), in the Libyan Arab Jamahiriya and in Norway;

— a loan from public funds: in Norway;

— total or partial exemption from certain taxes and customs duties: in Belgium, Brazil, the United Republic of Cameroon, the Congo, Denmark, the Federal Republic of Germany, Italy, Madagascar, Switzerland;

— the granting of special rates by the postal services, the telecommunications services or the railways: the United Republic of Cameroon, Finland, Honduras, Italy, Madagascar, Norway (where the Government assumes charges for communications between provincial newspapers and the capital to compensate for the handicap they face on account of the configuration of the country), Switzerland;

— advertising aid, by which the State guarantees the press a part of its own advertising (Barbados, Norway) or sets aside for the press a tax from advertising expenditure (in Costa Rica, the revenue from this tax partly finances the journalists' union and the school of journalism at the university).

This study is not the place to give a value judgement on the possible impact these economic measures by the State may have on the freedom of the press. Neither will it seek to determine whether public aid really works to the advantage of the newspapers or their readers. It is sufficient to conclude that, as shown by Sweden, this aid has certainly ensured the survival of many newspapers and, by the same token, the employment of much of their staff.

EXTENT OF UNEMPLOYMENT AMONG JOURNALISTS

In the press, as in other sectors, structural changes and technological evolution are a threat to employment, not only for printing workers but also for editorial staff — although in a different way and to a lesser extent. Moreover, as has been noted, the new line followed by a newspaper after a merger or change of owner can result in journalists leaving without any certainty of finding an editorial post with another publication.

A further reason for unemployment which is often mentioned is the disproportionately large number of candidates in journalism. There are two causes for this: the attraction of the profession and the significant development in training methods, both of which encourage too great a number of applicants for the press in certain countries to absorb. For example, the National Federation of Professional Journalists in Brazil has no doubt that the increasing unemployment among its members is due to the current lack of balance between the stagnating labour market in press businesses and the rapid expansion in the training of journalists in the universities. A number of countries avoid this imbalance by restricting access to training, thus diverting unemployment risks towards other professions: this is the case in Australia where a very selective admission system in the initial stage means that the press labour market can be controlled at source. In other countries, however, the unemployment of young graduates is a serious problem for the profession of journalism, as it is in other professions where the attraction is strong enough to make the student blind to the possibility of there being more candidates than there are openings. The extent of this problem is difficult to evaluate since unemployment figures do not normally distinguish, by profession, the number of persons seeking a first job and many fresh graduates go into other occupations while waiting for an editorial post; at least, such is their hope.

Staff journalists are vulnerable to the repercussions of certain difficulties which affect printing personnel. The latter may have certain reasons for entering into conflict with the newspaper management. As has been seen, printing staff are the most directly affected by the adoption of the new technology and sometimes react in a way that paralyses the newspaper for a long time and can reduce the editorial staff to a state of technical unemployment. Prolonged strikes by press delivery services can have similar consequences.

The closing of newspapers for political reasons is another cause of unemployment. Contemporary history is littered with such examples. Journalists who have been the victims of these measures often have great trouble in finding another job in their profession, since the restrictions that have led to the closing down of a newspaper generally make it difficult for the journalists to find work in other sections of the press.

Profession: Journalist

Despite all this, many countries which replied to an ILO questionnaire stated that unemployment among journalists was non-existent or negligible. Some even declared that there were shortages of staff, especially of sub-editors (Australia and New Zealand).

However, others indicate latent unemployment (Costa Rica) or increasing unemployment (Brazil). In Iraq, it is only apparent in the private sector. In Italy, it affects 400 persons out of a total of 6,000. In Denmark, it is in about the same proportion: on 1 August 1978, the Union of Journalists noted that of its 3,561 members, 236 were out of work, i.e. 6.6 per cent of the total; 67 were less than 30 years of age, 109 from 30 to 50 years of age, and 60 were above 50 years of age; 77 had been without a job for less than three months, 18 from three to six months, 45 between six and 12 months and 96 for more than one year; the percentage of unemployed had remained more or less stable since April 1977.

France is the country where the situation is the most worrying. The journalists' unions estimated that in 1978, of a total 15,500 professional journalists, 2,750 were out of work (that is, nearly 18 per cent). However, the unions gave no explanation as to the factors which might make the profession more vulnerable in France than in other countries.

The Swiss Federation of Journalists knew of no unemployment due to economic causes at that time, but felt that the situation could change overnight if a publication ceased to exist. But the Federation also noted that there was a measure of partial unemployment among independent journalists, the natural victims of economic measures taken by newspapers.

The above comment is probably valid in all countries and certainly gives a false impression of unemployment statistics: the freelance journalist plays the role of a shock absorber, easy to recruit when things are going well, just as easily dropped in hard times. As independent workers, freelance journalists are not recognised in many systems of unemployment insurance. And in cases where they could claim an allowance, they often do so only after months of fruitless effort to find a job.

It would therefore seem that, in addition to new graduates, freelance journalists are currently the principal victims of unemployment in the profession. Does this mean that the many countries in which there is no unemployment in this field will remain immune to it? In particular, will they do so if the tendency towards concentration speeds up? Will the advent of new technology have graver effects on the employment of journalists than those caused to date through photocomposition? The progress made in transmitting news and pictures has already reduced the need for reporters. Even more serious for the future is the question of how newspapers will face up to the development of electronic methods of communicating information. What will happen to press markets when every home can be linked to a data bank and summon on to its television screen — which already provides general information, and, in the case of cable television, local information — a continuous variety of information? The danger is that these markets will crumble away to a level where they are no longer viable. And will the jobs created by these new methods provide enough jobs for journalists?

These are the questions likely to challenge all those involved in the various processes of daily newspaper production, from the arrival of the news on the teleprinter to packaging and dispatch, and those who wonder how and why a mechanism so well lubricated and so well adapted to meeting an obvious public need could ever cease to exist. These questions are now beginning to arouse more attention. It is essential that those responsible for the future of the profession be aware that a major transformation is under way.

Notes

[1] See in particular Michel Logié: "L'imprimerie de presse en évolution", in *Cahiers français* (Paris), Oct.-Dec. 1976, pp. 21-27; Royal Commission on the Press: *New technology and the press: A study of experience in the United States*, by Rex Winsbury (London, HMSO, 1975); ILO: *Technological developments and their implications for employment in the printing and allied trades, with particular reference to developing countries*, Report III, Second Tripartite Technical Meeting for the Printing and Allied Trades, Geneva, 1981; Rex Winsbury: *New technologies in newspaper production in developing countries and their labour and social implications* (Geneva, ILO, 1981; mimeographed World Employment Programme research working paper; restricted).

[2] Louis Guéry: "Dans l'entreprise moderne, qui fera quoi?", in *Avenirs* (Paris, Office national d'information sur les enseignements et les professions), Oct.-Nov. 1976, pp. 54-56.

[3] From 36 to 62 per cent depending on the newspapers, according to the Royal Commission on the Press: *Final report*, op. cit., p. 42.

[4] Royal Commission on the Press: *New technology and the press ...*, op. cit., pp. 9-10.

[5] Rex Winsbury: *New technologies in newspaper production ...*, op. cit., p. 8.

[6] See "L'agence France-Presse", in *Notes et études documentaires* (Paris, La documentation française), Nos. 4336-4337, 23 Nov. 1976, pp. 40-45.

[7] Royal Commission on the Press: *New technology and the press ...*, op. cit., pp. 52-53.

[8] *Direct Line* (Brussels, International Federation of Journalists (IFJ)), Sep. 1978, pp. 2-3.

[9] ibid., June 1980, pp. 3-4.

[10] *Social and Labour Bulletin* (Geneva, ILO), No. 2/78, pp. 143-144.

[11] ibid., No. 3/81, pp. 251-252.

[12] *Direct Line*, Oct. 1981.

[13] *The Democratic Journalist* (Prague, International Organisation of Journalists), No. 1-80, p. 15.

[14] *Direct Line*, July-Aug. 1980.

[15] ibid., Mar. 1978.

[16] The agreement at *The Times*, which, on 20 October 1979, ended 11 months of conflict, reserves the use of the computer to print workers, but it is understood that the matter will be re-examined at a later date yet to be specified.

[17] *Free Labour World* (Brussels, International Confederation of Free Trade Unions), Sep.-Oct. 1978, pp. 29-30.
[18] *Social and Labour Bulletin*, No. 4/80, pp. 381-383.
[19] *Direct Line*, Mar. 1979.
[20] *Social and Labour Bulletin*, No. 2/80, pp. 143-145.
[21] Newspaper revenues in the United Kingdom in 1980 showed the following breakdown: sales, 42 per cent; advertising, 58 per cent (*Financial Times* (London), 20 Oct. 1981).
[22] Y. Lavoinne: *La presse* (Paris, Librairie Larousse, 1976), p. 91.
[23] *Massen-Medien in Österreich* (Vienna, Internationale Publikationen Gesellschaft, 1977), p. 55.
[24] "La presse quotidienne", in *Cahiers français* (Paris), Oct.-Dec. 1978, p. 48.
[25] W. A. Mahle and R. Richter: *Communication policies in the Federal Republic of Germany* (Paris, UNESCO Press, 1974), pp. 39 and 75,
[26] "La presse quotidienne", op. cit., p. 50.
[27] ACAS, op. cit., p. 222.
[28] Royal Commission on the Press: *Final report*, op. cit., p. 25.
[29] *John Herling's Labor Letter* (Washington, DC), 3 Feb. 1979.
[30] S. B. Chung: "Presse et information au Japon", in *Problèmes politiques et sociaux* (Paris, La documentation française), No. 303, 4 Feb. 1977, p. 4.
[31] "La presse quotidienne", op. cit., p. 45.

ETHICAL STANDARDS IN THE PROFESSION 4

Though comparatively brief, this chapter deals with one of the main problems of the journalist as a worker: practice of the profession implies respect for certain values (ethical, religious, professional, etc.) and the journalist who wishes to remain faithful to these values in working relationships is confronted with specific problems. The question at issue is the protection of the journalist's legitimate rights as a worker and the determination of the special obligations incumbent upon the employer.

In the past, some attention has been given to the nature and classification of the ethical standards of journalism. But this is not the case in an area which concerns the ILO in particular: the need for protection, which is a counterpart of the right to work. The conscience clause, which was examined within the ILO before the Second World War, is dealt with below. But it goes without saying that other problems deserve at least equal attention. This especially applies to the kind of protection the journalist should have so far as the demands of professional secrecy are concerned.

CODES OF ETHICS

Codes of ethics exist under different names in many countries: [1] codes of honour, codes of the press, declarations of the rights and obligations of the journalist, charters of professional obligations, canons of journalism, etc. Whatever their titles may be, the contents of the rules in these codes are extremely varied. However, most of the codes have certain features in common, particularly those concerning the primary function of the press to inform and to inform correctly: in this respect, the journalist has an obligation to defend the freedom and independence of information and comment, although it is understood that these two areas must remain distinct; to abide by the truth and consequently to avoid bias of the news through partisan or misleading presentation; to check the veracity of the information; to publish any necessary corrections; to preserve professional secrecy; and not to divulge information sources (although a number of countries do not recognise the latter obligation). Other obligations are more on the level of elementary moral considerations: to refrain from slander, libel or the disclosure of private lives; to avoid debasing the standards of "public morals" by taking a lenient view of violence or vice; and to abstain from unfair methods (e.g. hiding one's identity as a journalist) in order to obtain information. Other considerations relate to solidarity between journalists — mutual assistance and a ban on plagiarism and unfair competition.

In some codes, these obligations also imply rights. Those most often mentioned are freedom of access to information sources, the right to investigate freely all matters concerning public life and the right of journalists to refuse professional activity which may be contrary to their convictions or conscience. The much-discussed "conscience clause", and its repercussions in the event of termination of contract, will be examined below.

Some of the ethical codes have been drawn up by the public authorities. This is the case in Italy where a law dated 3 February 1963, which founded an institute of journalists, summarises the rights and obligations of journalists, establishes the register of journalists referred to in Chapter 1 and specifies the penalties (warnings, censorship, suspension, being struck off the register) which can be imposed on those who act contrary to the honour and dignity of the profession. It should be added, however, that the National Press Council has formulated principles for the ethical behaviour and self-discipline of professional journalists, the application of which is supervised by a tribunal. In the United Republic of Cameroon, the press law of 21 December 1966 contains various points on ethical standards, such as the obligation of publishers of material for young people to avoid stories or illustrations which may present any crime or offence in a favourable light and the prohibition of the advocacy of magic, witchcraft, occultism or pornography. The decree of 21 March 1974 setting up a press charter in Madagascar enumerates the duties and obligations of a "journalist worthy of the name"; it also provides for the creation of an institute of journalists in which all journalists should be registered and which is responsible for the creation and application of an ethical code; the institute was finally created by decree on 27 March 1974. In Sri Lanka, the Press Council law of 27 February 1973 contains a number of ethical rules and provides for the creation of a code of conduct for journalists.

But it is obviously the profession itself which defines its own ethical standards in most countries.

In many countries, journalists' associations or unions have spontaneously assumed the task of formulating their own list of obligations. Among these are Australia, Canada, Colombia, Egypt, Finland, France,

Hungary, India, Indonesia, Ireland, Jamaica, New Zealand, Nicaragua, Nigeria, Norway, Sweden, Switzerland, the United Kingdom, the United States, Venezuela and Yugoslavia.

Prompted by the same concern to specify the primary obligations of journalists without outside intervention, the International Federation of Journalists adopted its own code of honour, known as the Declaration of Bordeaux, in 1954. Later, in 1971, journalists' unions in the member countries of the European Community, at that time six in number, joined on this occasion by the journalists' unions in Austria and Switzerland, recapitulated this code of honour, expanding it on certain points and adding a statement of certain rights in a document known as The Declaration of Munich. Among other points, the two texts state that, where professional matters are concerned, journalists can only accept the jurisdiction of their peers, to the exclusion of all government or other interference.

The following examples illustrate the moral scope and limits of the codes set up by journalists themselves. In Australia, the ethical code forms part of the statutes of the Australian Journalists' Association; a committee composed of members of the Association examines complaints on code violations — incidentally quite rare (only a dozen in 1978). In France, the Charter of Obligations for Journalists, drawn up by the National Union of Journalists in 1938, is no more than a declaration of principle, since there is no body to control its application. The Declaration on the Obligations and Rights of Journalists adopted in 1972 by the Swiss Federation of Journalists was intended to be more binding, inasmuch as a press council was charged with ensuring its application; but this council, composed solely of journalists, was only set up at the end of 1977 and thus its effectiveness cannot yet be evaluated. The Nigerian Union of Journalists, whose code of conduct puts telling and respecting the truth as the first duty of a journalist, is particularly strict on this point; the Union takes every possible step to see that a journalist condemned for corruption by the national executive council of the Union is not allowed to practise as a journalist anywhere in the country.[2]

Clearly, no conclusions can be drawn from these isolated cases, but they would seem to indicate that the self-discipline and professional conscience of journalists are the best guarantees of the observance of the ethical standards which the journalists themselves or their peers have freely established, even if the standards are not supplemented by a disciplinary body or, conversely, are rarely applied. Moreover, the rejection of all outside interference, government or otherwise, as formulated in the Declarations of Bordeaux and Munich and in several national codes, is an additional incentive to self-discipline.

Certain associations of newspaper owners or publishers have felt it necessary to draw up a set of ethical rules to which journalists and other employees are equally subject. This is so in Burma, Chile, Denmark,

Japan, Pakistan and Turkey. In Japan, the Canons of Journalism, adopted in 1946 by the Japanese Newspaper Publishers' Association, were conceived by the authors as embracing all persons connected with journalistic activities. This code, together with those formulated by the Japanese Association of Magazine Publishers and by the National Commercial Radio Association in Japan, stresses the need for objectivity, impartiality, tolerance and decency and emphasises the cultural role and social responsibility of the media.

In other countries, the creation of ethical rules was the result of joint action by the two parties: publishers and journalists. This applies to Austria, Belgium, the Federal Republic of Germany, Israel, the Republic of Korea, Lebanon and Sweden. In the case of Sweden, the code adopted by the Swedish Journalists' Union has already been mentioned. But there were already a number of rules which had been jointly drawn up by the Publicists' Club, the Newspaper Publishers' Association and the Swedish Journalists' Union and these had found wide acceptance among journalists. In the Federal Republic of Germany, the Press Council, in collaboration with the two parties, drew up 15 Principles of Publication in 1973 and these in fact constitute a press code. The Austrian code, Directives for Publishing, is also the result of a joint effort by the Press Council and the two parties.

Certain clauses in a number of collective agreements also focus on matters of ethics and codes of conduct. For example, they are to be found in agreements made in Canada between the Newspaper Guild and various newspapers, in particular the clauses on non-disclosure, under the terms of which employers cannot compel employees to reveal their sources and must take measures to protect them against such demands from outside. The contract drawn up by the Newspaper Guild in the United States, updated at each of its negotiating conferences with newspapers and press agencies, contains similar measures. In France, the management agreement signed in 1978 within the AIGLE group (since dissolved) provided for the establishment of an editorial consultative council empowered to safeguard respect for ethical values and free to call on any professional journalist for advice in this area.

The press councils referred to above are responsible, among other duties, for maintaining a high standard of professional ethics. The first such council was set up in Sweden in 1916 but it is only recently that they have begun to proliferate: more than half of the 40 press councils now operating have been created since 1970.[3] These councils are for the most part joint bodies, consisting of representatives of publishers and journalists, with an independent chairman, generally an eminent retired judge. Several also have representatives of the public (the Province of Quebec in Canada, New Zealand, Norway, the United Kingdom) or of a public body (in India, universities, parliament, religious councils, the judiciary). In certain countries, the press council was set up by the public authorities (Indonesia), or solely by publishers (Denmark), or journalists (Switzerland). The powers of these councils are limited. They seldom go beyond identifying the culprit or censorship; some are not even able to impose penalties (Netherlands). In Sweden, the Press Council merely plays the role of a tribunal of honour. A press "ombudsman", usually a judge, examines public complaints or initiates action against press abuses; the ombudsman may also refer the complaint to the Press Council's Commission on Fair Practice.

It should be noted that the functions of press councils usually extend beyond the mere preservation of ethical standards. Their main role is to defend the freedom of the press. That is why they are sometimes described as a dog with two heads, one barking inside and the other outside. Some councils (the Federal Republic of Germany, the United Kingdom) are responsible for observing the structural evolution of the press, especially the trend towards concentration, and for making it known to the public; this task can also be considered as part of their effort to protect the freedom of the press.[4]

In summing up, it can be said that, as a professional group, journalists attach great importance to the observance of ethical standards. As proof of this, they have drawn up national codes of ethics, have participated in such work or have created press councils on which they are represented. The question now at issue is whether it is opportune or possible in practice to envisage international regulations on these matters. A special UNESCO body, the International Commission for the Study of Communication Problems, known as the MacBride Commission, has been studying the question. It seemed worth while to make the effort to identify common values, despite the diversity of social and political systems. The Commission found that it would probably be impossible to agree on a uniform set of professional standards, taking into account the existing different political and social systems.[5] However, in its final report, the majority opinion was that there were "no reasons to consider it unattainable or that its pursuit should be abandoned for reasons of principle" and that "it should at least be possible to reach agreement regarding practices from which the media should abstain".[6] In its recommendations, the Commission limited itself to stating that the adoption of professional codes of conduct "at national and, in some cases, at the regional level is desirable, provided that such codes are prepared and adopted by the profession itself without government interference".[7] Numerous journalists hold the opinion that the adoption of an international code of professional ethics is a matter which should be dealt with solely by the professional organisations concerned; others feel that debate on this subject only results in political controversy between non-professionals.

THE CONSCIENCE CLAUSE

Special attention should be given to a point which is to be found in a number of legislative or contractual texts: this is what is called "the conscience clause", an arrangement which, in the event of a change in newspaper policy, allows the journalist to resign without notice, or with the minimum of notice, and still retain the right to be paid compensation.

This clause corresponds to an age-old claim by the profession for recognition of the political, religious or moral views of its members in the exercise of their work.[8] The original International Federation of Journalists adopted this as a war cry at its first congress in 1926, but it was not until later that this clause was written into national legislation in a French law of 29 March 1935 (article 30 *d*, First Book of the Labour Code). This law stipulates that compensation for loss of employment is due to a journalist who breaks a work contract, if this break is caused by "an appreciable change in the character or trend of the newspaper or periodical, if this change places the employee in a situation likely to cast a slur upon his honour or reputation or to affect his moral interests in general". There must be two conditions: the change must be significant, affecting not only the political tone of the publication but also its information coverage; it must also be of a nature likely to prejudice the morals of the journalist.

The matter has been settled in much the same way in other countries, for example, Madagascar and Tunisia. Even when not set out so explicitly, considerations of this kind underlie the conscience clauses to be found in other legislation or collective agreements. Their texts strengthen the position of journalists either by removing or reducing their obligation to give notice, or by giving them the right to financial compensation, or even both. In brief, journalists are given the same rights when they resign on account of a policy change at the newspaper as if they were dismissed. In the Federal Republic of Germany, for example, journalists have the right to give notice as of the month during which they learn of the policy change, and to be paid compensation equal to the whole amount of their salary during the period of notice, and in any event at least for six months. In Austria, they can leave the newspaper on normal notice and they have the right to compensation based on their length of service, which means the equivalent of one year's salary if they have been there for five years or less, and one-and-a-half year's salary after five to ten years of service. The amount is increased by six months' salary for every five years of service after the first ten years. In Belgium and Finland, they can terminate their contract without notice and claim compensation equal to the amount they would have received if their employer had dismissed them. In Italy, if there is a basic change in the newspaper's policy, or if the publisher confronts journalists with a situation which is clearly incompatible with their professional dignity,

Ethical standards in the profession

they have the right to resign and to collect compensation for dismissal. In the Netherlands, they can reduce their notice period by half and collect between one month and one year's salary by way of compensation, depending on their length of service. In Switzerland, they have the right to leave the enterprise immediately and to receive compensation equal to four months' salary plus another month for each five years of service. In the French-speaking part of Switzerland, the compensation is equal to the salary which would be due after a normal period of notice. The collective agreement in this part of the country also specifies that journalists cannot be obliged to put their name to an article which is contrary to their convictions, but that they cannot oppose the publication of articles contrary to their own conviction (articles 5 and 6).

Yet it would be wrong to assume that the application of the conscience clause is a common practice. There are many countries where there are no provisions of this kind, as for example, Argentina, Denmark, the Republic of Korea, Luxembourg, Norway, Sweden and the United States. Moreover, the application of this clause is a delicate matter in practice.[9] As has been seen in the preceding chapter, the printed press is passing through a difficult period in many countries and there is a constant decrease in the number of newspapers. It takes courage even in normal times to resign from a job solely for ethical reasons, to give up a well-entrenched position with good prospects of career advancement and to turn one's back on intellectual and material comforts. In a time of crisis, with the risk of prolonged unemployment, if not the end of one's career, this amounts to an act of heroism. Nor is it an easy operation if the idea is to make the most of the financial advantages that, in principle, go with the conscience clause — that is, higher compensation than in the case of a normal resignation. It must be proved that there has really been a change of policy and that the change could prejudice the moral interests of the journalist; this is not an easy task since a policy change can often be quite subtle in the early stages and, consequently, the journalist may have to go through tortuous legal proceedings to prove the point. The conscience clause is a valuable part of the fabric of social welfare, but it is not the only issue which raises the question of personal convictions in the daily practice of the profession.

Notes

[1] See F. Geyer: *Les codes déontologiques dans la presse internationale* (Brussels, International Federation of Journalists, 1975; mimeographed); Lars Brunn: *Professional codes in journalism* (International Organisation of Journalists, 1979).

[2] *West Africa* (London), No. 3268, 10 Mar. 1980, p. 434.

[3] UNESCO, International Commission for the Study of Communication Problems: *Interim report* (Paris, 1978), para. 195.

⁴ See in particular Royal Commission on the Press: *Final report* (London, HMSO, 1977), p. 198.

⁵ UNESCO, International Commission for the Study of Communication Problems, International seminar at Stockholm (24-27 April 1978): *Infrastructure of news collection and dissemination*, p. 15.

⁶ The MacBride Commission: *Many voices, one world*, Report by the International Commission for the Study of Communication Problems (London, Kogan Page; New York, Unipub; Paris, UNESCO Press, 1980), p. 244.

⁷ ibid., p. 262.

⁸ The conscience clause is seldom mentioned in international legislation. It was not until 1977 that it appeared in an international labour instrument on working conditions, the Nursing Personnel Recommendation, 1977 (No. 157), couched in extremely prudent terms: "Nursing personnel should be able to claim exemption from performing specific duties, without being penalised, where performance would conflict with their religious, moral or ethical convictions and where they inform their supervisor in good time of their objection so as to allow the necessary arrangements to be made to ensure that essential nursing care of patients is not affected."

⁹ See P. Parisot and F. Périer Daville: "The protection of journalists", in *IFJ Information* (Brussels, International Federation of Journalists), Vol. XXX, 1980, pp. 14-15.

THE CAREER AND ITS PROBLEMS   5

There are some professions or sectors of activity which offer wide scope for advancement and where it is normally possible to avoid prolonged career stagnation.

For a number of reasons, this does not apply to journalism.

Most press enterprises are of modest size; with the exception of the big news agencies, which employ several hundred people, there are seldom more than a few dozen journalists. As a result, the chances of promotion are slender. Moreover, the modest financial resources of medium and small companies have a limiting effect on the collection and handling of news and, consequently, on the work of the journalists: the most that such newspapers can hope to do is to publish dispatches from news agencies and local correspondents, without rewriting, refining or expanding them. For example, New Zealand newspapers are usually small concerns which are privately financed and which, for lack of material resources, tend to record events and conferences rather than to practise any investigative reporting. The result is that journalists who want to produce original work and to advance in their careers are somewhat frustrated.

Even in more powerful press organisations, career prospects are limited because there are only a few ranks in the hierarchy. The jobs may be diversified but they are only on a few levels, and to get from one level to the next is generally a slow and uncertain process, even if there is nothing in principle to prevent a young journalist from one day becoming the editor. This explains why, apart from progression up the hierarchy or promotion, bonuses for long service and systems of advancement, which are automatic in some countries and press groups but not necessarily so in others, have been introduced.

Profession: Journalist

RECRUITMENT

This section concentrates on the conditions of training required for employment. In effect, they correspond to those required for access to the profession.

The formal conditions required for access to journalism have already been referred to. Generally it can be said that there are some countries where access is free and others where it is subject to certain conditions, especially with regard to the level of education required.

By way of example, the Federal Republic of Germany is in the first category. There, free access is a basic principle and no diploma is needed, at least in theory. In Barbados, France,[1] Hong Kong, Japan, Sweden and Switzerland, recruitment is not subject to any basic principles beyond those applicable under the general labour regulations.

In other countries, a minimum level of education or training is required. It has been noted above, for example, that Australian cadets must have the Higher School Certificate, and that Italian trainees are not entered on the register of journalists until they have undergone a test in general culture. In Brazil, under the terms of decree No. 972 of 17 October 1969, journalists can practise their profession only if they have obtained a diploma from an official higher education establishment or from one recognised for diplomas in journalism. In Egypt, under the press law of 1970 (No. 76), only university graduates can enter the profession. In Guyana, it is essential to have the "O"-Level General Certificate of Education in three to five subjects which can be taken after four years of secondary studies. In Ireland, in the case of Dublin newspapers, a diploma in journalism or a university degree is required or, alternatively, experience on provincial newspapers. In Liberia, the theoretical minimum is an intermediate degree, but in practice the normal criterion applied is the ability to write well in English. In Nigeria, all new entrants are obliged to follow the courses at the Institute of Journalists before being allowed to work in the profession.[2] In New Zealand, recruitment is made on the basis of preparatory courses designed for future cadets, although some newspapers take trainees directly from secondary schools. In Poland, recruits are drawn from students in faculties of journalism or from other specialised fields; secondary school candidates are not admitted, particularly for technical jobs, unless they undertake higher studies. In the United Kingdom, the agreement between the Newspaper Society and the two journalists' unions stipulates as a minimum condition that candidates must have the "O"-Level General Certificate of Education with a C grade (or higher) in five subjects, one of which must be English.[3] The national collective agreement on press undertakings in Tunisia defines the conditions for access to various posts: for example, an editor must have two years of higher education or five years of service in the category below that of editor; employers must conduct professional tests for all vacant posts.

In a number of African countries, as mentioned earlier, journalists, or at least some of them, are civil servants. Candidates for such posts must therefore meet the conditions laid down for entry into the public service or the special conditions for access to this kind of work. Thus, in the United Republic of Cameroon, decree No. 75-769 of 18 December 1975, concerning the special status of information officials, describes the methods of access to various posts (senior journalist, journalist, assistant journalist) as follows: by merit, by way of professional competition or by promotion; it specifies the breakdown for each of these three methods of recruitment as well as the diplomas required for admission on merit. In the Congo, decree No. 75/338 of 19 July 1975, concerning general regulations for the information services, lists the diplomas required for each grade. In the Ivory Coast, under the special regulations concerning staff of the Ivory Coast radio and television service, the sub-editors, reporters and cameramen of this organisation are recruited solely by competition open only to candidates holding a higher diploma in journalism granted by a recognised school or by one approved by the Government.

Even in countries where access to the profession is not subject to the holding of a diploma, it is obvious that employers tend to give preference, all things being equal, to candidates with superior intellectual qualities. At the same time, would-be journalists seek to increase their chances of entering the profession by acquiring further university qualifications. Thus, although Agence France-Presse does not ask for any diploma, it does in fact do its recruiting at the Training Centre for Journalists in Paris or the Advanced School of Journalism in Lille, and its staff includes many graduates in law, literature, history, geography, politics and economics, as well as former students of the *grandes écoles*.[4]

As to recruitment methods, leaving aside the strict rules applicable in some countries on the recruitment of journalists holding the status of civil servant or similar, an empirical approach would appear to be the rule. Employers very often recruit journalists through classified advertisements or personal recommendation and occasionally they canvass specialised schools. The methods used by candidates are job applications, letters to newspapers, personal recommendation or requests via their schools. The next step is the interview or, as in Japan, an open competition organised by the media. Normally, the engagement is only confirmed after a period of probation, which is subject to a number of collective agreements, or after a period of training.

This empirical approach would appear to be unaffected in most places by the laws of supply and demand. In certain countries, the profession itself tries to keep the balance. For example, in the preamble to the national agreement for the provincial press in the United Kingdom, it is stated: "it is essential for the intake into the industry to be adequate for its needs at all times and it is the declared intention that the intake shall not be of such proportions as to prejudice the training of juniors or lead to redundancy". Respecting the numerical proportions between trainees and qualified journalists — as mentioned in some of the texts quoted above — might maintain the balance within the profession if observed in practice, but it still leaves unresolved the problem of young people looking for jobs. Employment agencies have practically no impact where journalists are concerned. In France, for example, the National Association for Employment (ANPE) has a public monopoly for placing staff. The Labour Code makes it obligatory for all workers seeking a job to register with the agency and for all employers to notify vacancies to the agency (article L. 311-2). The national collective agreement for journalists echoes this obligation. It invites employers to seek first among "professional journalists temporarily out of work or working only part time, or those who have been trained in establishments recognised by the profession ... the collaborator suited for the post available" (article 12). But in reality, press enterprises have wide freedom to hire at will. Similar clauses appear in the collective agreement in Senegal (article 11), but the wording is too vague for it to affect the freedom of the employer on this matter.

ADVANCEMENT AND MOBILITY IN THE PROFESSION

Promotion

Many contractual agreements and regulations deal with promotion. Some of them, such as the national collective agreements in Poland and Tunisia, or the statutes for public service journalists in the United Republic of Cameroon, the Congo and Madagascar, provide for the conditions of access to various posts in the hierarchy. The Tunisian agreement specifies the diplomas and length of service required in the lower ranks to progress from editorial assistant to editor, passing successively through the posts of reporter, sub-editor, chief reporter, chief sub-editor, deputy editor first or second grade. It also stipulates certain conditions required for access to a key post: the section head must have at least the rank of editor and the department head that of chief reporter. The same document sets out the general criteria, in addition to the special criteria that have been mentioned, which govern promotion — that is, length of active service in the profession, professional training and aptitude, length of service and performance record in the establishment and family responsibilities. Total length of service is considered on three levels: in the category, in the establishment itself, and in the profession.

The career and its problems

In the texts of most agreements, the criteria for promotion are set out in general terms. Length of service, competence and efficiency are the usual factors taken into account, but it is frequently pointed out that, in the final analysis, it is up to the employer to judge. It is also often recommended that, when a vacancy comes up, journalists already working in the department concerned should be given priority. Another proposal sometimes made is that the higher post should be filled on a provisional basis on condition that, after a fixed period, the person concerned be confirmed in that post.

In many instances, there is provision for a trial period in the new post, it being understood that if the journalist's performance is not satisfactory, or the journalist prefers not to accept the new post, he or she will be reintegrated in the previous job without prejudice.

As can be supposed, ongoing training and promotion are closely linked. The importance given in the agreements to professional competence and the possession of diplomas as criteria for promotion is, among other factors, a strong inducement to those journalists who are ambitious to move up in the hierarchy to improve their all-round knowledge and qualifications.

Moving up the ladder, service bonuses

Even when journalists make this effort and when their professional qualifications are excellent, their progression in the hierarchy is subject to many variables. The scarcity of vacancies, the great number of highly talented colleagues and the fact that they have a family or other commitments which might restrict mobility, not to mention other factors of a non-professional nature (politics, for example) which can influence the choice of the employer, often condemn the journalist to prolonged stagnation. Moving up in rank and bonuses for long service are certainly a palliative for the frustrations caused by such stagnation.

In France, salary scales for different grades in certain categories take into account a career profile in the same job, for want of a genuine career record as demanded by the unions. To this can be added service bonuses, which are of two kinds and are calculated on the basis of length of service in the profession and in the enterprise. Journalists with a career of 20 years in the profession receive a bonus equal to 11 per cent of the basic salary for their category and rank. If they have 20 years of service in the same enterprise, they also receive a bonus of 9 per cent; if they move to another company, they retain their professional career bonus. Similarly, in Italy, basic salaries also carry a long-service bonus which increases for every two years of service with the same company and in the same category. In New Zealand, after three years as a cadet, journalists benefit from an automatic system of advancement by which they move up eight rungs of the ladder in eight years. Those who complete the preparatory courses mentioned above are credited with a certain additional period of service: six months for those who studied in Auckland, one year for those who studied in Wellington and two years for university graduates. After reaching the eighth rung of the ladder, promotion is based on merit. In the United Kingdom, the agreement concluded at Reuters news agency stipulates that advancement in the same grade is by way of automatic salary increases, except when the employer wishes to accelerate the promotion of a certain journalist or, conversely, when there have been unfavourable reports on a journalist's work.

Automatic advancement is thus a feature of these systems. In certain cases, however, the system has defects: in Australia, for example, where journalists are classified into six grades (in descending order: A special, A.2, A, B, C, and D), a journalist considered as talented normally goes from grade D to C in 12 to 18 months and from C to B in one or two years. Subsequent advancement depends on the journalist's abilities and opportunities for promotion.

A further cause of frustration in this profession, as in many others, is that the workers constantly feel that their jobs are not properly classified and that they are therefore not correctly paid. In most press undertakings, anomalies of this type, real or assumed, can be individually negotiated. In certain countries there are formal claim procedures for this type of situation. The collective agreement for professional journalists in Senegal allows journalists to lodge a claim with their employer, directly or through a staff representative. If they fail to obtain satisfaction, they can appeal to the Professional Commission on Classification. This Commission, chaired by the inspector of labour and made up of two employers' representatives and two workers' representatives, votes by majority. If one of the parties rejects the decision, the dispute goes before the labour tribunal (article 14).

Grades

Systems for promotion in the job hierarchy and normal progress from one rank to another are often subject to a grading process. It is not surprising that this procedure is applied to journalists who have civil service, or similar, status. But the same procedure is also to be found in the private sector. For example, the collective agreement of Associated Press in the United States stipulates that all employees' work must be reviewed at least once a year. On request and after discussion with their section chief, employees are informed of the evaluation made of them and have the right to see the written report in their personal files; the employer supplies the union with a nominal list of merit rises (articles

The career and its problems

VI.9 and XIV.1 of the 1976-78 agreement). Under the Reuters agreement of 1978, in the United Kingdom, a report on the work of each journalist, based on information supplied by the news-desk chief and a colleague familiar with the work of, and senior in rank to, the journalist concerned, is prepared annually. The journalist reads the report and may comment on it in writing; in that event, the author of the report may choose to add further comments or modify the evaluation; the final text must again be communicated to the interested party (article 11). Under the terms of the national collective agreement in Tunisia, all journalists are given an overall grading once a year, numbered from 0 to 20. The grade is based on their performance, professional know-how, application, behaviour and punctuality, as well as on a general evaluation which indicates their chances of promotion; the authority to grant grades lies with the head of the company who consults the hierarchical superior of each person concerned; and journalists can request an advancement commission to intervene with a view to a revision of their grading (article 10).

Professional mobility

When journalists fail to find the career satisfaction they had hoped for within their own press organisation, they have no other choice but to look elsewhere. Other reasons may also induce them to look outside: the closure of their newspaper, regrouping of editorial staff, internal reorganisation, or disagreement with the policy of the newspaper.[5] If their job is eliminated or modified to a point beyond which they cannot continue, or if someone else takes it over, the result is resignation or dismissal. The simple attraction of the new and unknown, always a powerful magnet in this profession, can also play a role in mobility.

Whatever the cause may be, journalists will turn to another section of the press or perhaps to another type of activity.

Naturally, going to another newspaper is what usually happens. This can also mean a *de facto* promotion. A typical example in this context is the tradition mentioned earlier by which, in the United Kingdom, it is nearly impossible to move up to a job in the national press without having acquired experience on provincial newspapers. An agreement signed in 1965 between the Newspaper Publishers Association and the National Union of Journalists prohibits Fleet Street newspapers — the place where most of the major London newspapers are concentrated — from recruiting newcomers to journalism, apart from a limited number of specialists each year, except from the provincial press.

There are many other types of activity which attract journalists. The most common are those associated with journalism: press officer in large industrial or commercial concerns or in government departments, for example; others are in advertising, public relations and, naturally, the whole field of politics. The old saying "journalism opens up all doors" is largely true.

ADVANCED TRAINING

The nature of the job performed by the journalist means that advanced training on the job is both essential and relatively easy.

Since journalists must inform readers and enlighten public opinion, they are obliged at all times to expand and deepen their own knowledge. This is particularly true for those who work in specialised fields such as science and technology, as they are expected to provide expert and reliable information on the evolution of theories and on their practical applications. Journalists must also adapt themselves to changes in style which affect the presentation of news, from both the production and the writing point of view. The revolutionary changes in printing techniques also have an effect on their work, as has been seen in Chapter 3, and oblige journalists to keep abreast of methods previously unknown in the profession.

By virtue of the job, journalists are remarkably well placed to communicate their knowledge. The regular practice of most professions is in itself a means of acquiring further knowledge in the field concerned. It is certainly true of journalism: those whose task it is to inform are constantly informing themselves. Moreover, the atmosphere in which journalists work is in itself conducive to this daily enrichment, for being in a newspaper is virtually cultural immersion: archives and libraries are an inexhaustible mine of information and the continual exchanges within an editorial department devoted entirely to research and to the communication of information stimulate intellectual curiosity and enrich background knowledge.

However, all this must be taken a step further with a view to acquiring knowledge and applying it systematically. This is a matter of personal initiative, but also calls for participation by the public authorities, the profession itself and the teaching institutions.

Personal initiative, in any case indispensable, is up to the individual in certain countries. In Australia, for example, once they have passed the cadet stage, journalists wishing to continue their training do so at their own expense and in their free time. Similarly, in the United Republic of Cameroon, further training is above all a personal matter and is done on the job. Retraining courses involve only a small number of journalists. In countries where advanced courses for journalists are not regulated by law or under contract, it is obviously up to those concerned to take the necessary steps themselves if they wish to progress beyond the stage of their normal working experience: for example, taking university courses and negotiating suitable working hours and leave with their employers.

Public authorities do intervene in the area of refresher courses for journalists through legislation on further training and by contributing to the expenses involved. Some examples are given below.

In the Federal Republic of Germany, the federal and state governments grant financial support to institutions teaching journalism. Occasionally, the Central Federal Office for Civic Education organises seminars for editors of local newspapers on subjects such as community management and regional planning.[6] However, the purpose of these is not so much to train journalists as to use the press as a medium for communicating objective information on matters of local interest to the public.

Under the law in Bulgaria,[7] journalists who follow correspondence courses have the right to educational leave of 30 days per school year in order to attend courses which require their presence and to prepare for and take their exams. For those attending an educational establishment while doing their job, educational leave is six days annually per school year and 12 days in the year when they complete their studies; they also have the right to 20 extra days to prepare for and sit their exams (30 days for a state examination) and 100 days to prepare and present a thesis.

Like all other employees in France, journalists benefit from the law of 1971 on further training. Under the terms of this law, all employers with a minimum of ten salaried employees must participate in financing training schemes, either by direct contributions or by payments to approved establishments. Further training generally takes the form of courses and special educational leave. In certain circumstances, the State itself reimburses the company a part of the remuneration paid to trainees. In cases where their contract does not provide for remuneration, the State pays compensation to trainees. According to the General Union of Journalists, affiliated to the *Force ouvrière (Syndicat général des journalistes/Force ouvrière)*, the application of the law, at least in the beginning, met with a certain reticence on the part of press companies which feared that their staffs would be reduced through these courses and through time off for training; it also encountered indifference among many journalists, but now its purpose seems to be better understood.

In New Zealand, continuous training, refresher courses or advanced training courses tend to take the form of regional seminars organised by the Journalists Training Board. They deal with such subjects as legal and sports reporting and the coverage of a general election.

In the USSR,[8] the law states that journalists who attend general education courses at night are entitled to a reduction in working hours and 36 days' leave per school year at half-pay; the employer can release them from service for one or two further days per week, but without pay. Special paid leave of variable duration is granted to them to sit for matriculation or the university entrance examination. Similar and even better arrangements are made for higher examinations. Newspapers grant their most talented collaborators paid leave for "creative work".

But it is obviously the profession itself which, with or without the support of the public authorities, plays the principal role in developing the qualifications of journalists. It does so either through the application of collective agreements or through initiatives taken by either publishers or journalists.

The national collective agreement on the work of journalists in the French press is an example of an agreement which contains clauses on further professional training. It underlines the importance of further training which is designed to enable journalists to exploit or expand their general knowledge in order to improve their cultural and professional level; to acquire deeper insight in a specific area connected with their activities; to receive new training leading to new assignments in their company, to enable them to adapt to new techniques and to prepare them for a change of profession. The document invites press enterprises to encourage the signing of agreements with a view to the creation and development of insurance-training funds, set up and managed on the basis of joint representation, at all press levels (article 9).

Numerous company agreements in the United Kingdom [9] provide for leave for training, usually four weeks after each four or five years of service. It is normally stipulated that this leave must not be taken during the holiday season. The 1977 agreement at *The Times* defined the purpose of this sabbatical leave for journalists: "to take a break for intellectual refreshment and to gain additional experience or knowledge relevant to their professional duties". It provided for study bursaries but prohibited any work for another newspaper during this period (article 15).

The collective agreement for professional journalists in Senegal obliges the employer to set up a permanent training fund, financed by proprietors to the tune of 1 per cent of the total of salaries paid to journalists. This fund is designed to allow journalists to take refresher and information courses and to organise local courses for the benefit of professionals (article 43).

In Sweden, the training organised by the Committee for the Further Training of Journalists at the State College of Kalmar is regulated by a joint agreement between the Swedish Journalists' Union and the Newspaper Publishers' Association. The college offers staff journalists on dailies with small or medium circulations short courses on subjects of direct interest to them; as of the fiscal year 1978-79, the Committee for the Further Training of Journalists has been responsible for familiarising journalists with the new technology. The State pays travel and lodging expenses and the employer continues to pay the participants their normal salary.

In Switzerland, the question of further training is regulated by contract in companies subject to the collective agreement between the

The career and its problems

Swiss Association of Newspaper Publishers and the Swiss Federation of Journalists (FSJ) or to the agreement between the Newspaper Union of French-speaking Switzerland and the FSJ. The latter agreement entrusts the setting up of these training courses to the joint commission which was mentioned in the preceding section; financing is provided by a contribution calculated according to the basic salary of each journalist and is paid in equal amounts by the journalist and the publisher. The joint commission may organise courses open to all active members of the FSJ who register for them of their own volition; to this end, the journalist is entitled to four half-days annually. In addition, each publication creates an internal committee for further training. The available options are internal courses, individual programmes and leave for training. The agreement signed in 1978 by the Swiss Federation of Public Services and the Socialist Press Union of Aargau guarantees journalists one week's leave a year for training.

Under the terms of article 33 of the national collective agreement of 1975 concerning press enterprises in Tunisia, the employer is to take all necessary steps to enable his workers to undertake training and further professional training in co-operation with the joint commission.

The scope and nature of the further training activities for professionals undertaken by publishers, either to implement legislative or contractual obligations (as has been described above in the case of the French press), or independently of such obligations, naturally varies from one country to another and from one section of the press to another.

In the Federal Republic of Germany, for example, radio stations have set up a central office for advanced training of radio programme staff. Its task is to draw up programmes for such staff (including journalists) and to control and co-ordinate them. No such instrument is available to journalists on the printed press.

The National Press Centre of the Libyan Arab Jamahiriya, one of whose main objectives is to encourage the "Libyanisation" of people working in journalism, organises numerous courses — some of which welcome citizens from other Arab countries — which concentrate on various aspects of the profession, such as page make-up. Trainees are also sent abroad, particularly to the United Kingdom, but priority is given to training within the country.

Some of the main sections of the Japanese press provide systematic further training for their staff; others rely on the daily experience accumulated by journalists and their own personal efforts. Radio and television stations set up various types of further training courses, ranging from simple language courses to "residential" courses which embrace a wide range of subjects and take place every four or five years.

A New Zealand daily newspaper sponsors seminars for press photographers as well as an annual course of two weeks for sub-editors.

Profession: Journalist

The journalists' unions play an active role in some countries in further training programmes. For example, the Bulgarian Union of Journalists organises language courses in a seaside resort; the courses last six months and the participants, released from service, continue to receive their normal salary. The same union has established a creative fund for financing leave of absence and missions for journalists engaged in long-term creative work.[10] The Polish Union of Journalists has its own centre which provides seminars on selected themes, language courses and practical exercises; it also organises journalists' clubs which provide facilities for various forms of advanced training. In the USSR, many local sections of the Union of Journalists have their own training and further training institute: in Moscow, more than 500 employees of newspapers, news agencies, magazines, etc., study in the different departments of institutes of this kind.[11]

The further training activities sponsored by the International Organisation of Journalists [12] should not be overlooked. These take the form of seminars or discussions on topical problems in the media, or longer courses in the IOJ's three international centres at Budapest, Berlin and Prague.

Teaching institutions play a major role in the advanced professional training of journalists. Whether public authorities, employers or trade union organisations help them or not, working journalists naturally turn to such institutions when they decide to improve their professional qualifications, particularly when such facilities are not available through their enterprises or unions. This is obviously true of establishments which provide a general education or courses in an area in which the journalist has specialised, provided that the journalist meets the required conditions of admission. It is even more true of the specialised schools: faculties or institutes of journalism attached to universities, or independent schools.

Certain institutions organise further training programmes specially designed for journalists, or make special arrangements for them. For example, Columbia University of New York offers professional journalists bursaries (scholarships) with which they can follow a one-year study course on economics and finance; once they have completed the course, they return to their publication and specialise in economics. The School of Journalism in Stockholm has recently started to offer working journalists six-month courses which enable them to extend their knowledge on a specific social question. The topic can vary from one course to another, and might be, for example, the economy and the labour market, or the environment and social planning. In France, the Advanced Training Centre for Journalists and Editorial Staff, created in 1969 under the joint sponsorship of the Centre of Training for Journalists in Paris and the Advanced School of Journalism in Lille, has taken up the challenge presented by the modernisation of the industry. The Centre has met with a favourable reaction, since in ten years the number of listening hours has risen from 25,700 to 130,000.[13] This would seem to confirm the evidence cited above that interest in the laws governing further professional training is increasing within the profession. The sessions at the Centre aim at the updating of knowledge and the acquisition of skills in the various techniques: training of sub-editors prior to the introduction of photocomposition, journalistic writing, news photography, etc.; some courses are specially designed for those writing specialist columns on such subjects as computers and telematics.

EQUALITY OF OPPORTUNITY BETWEEN MEN AND WOMEN

As has been seen in Chapter 2, women are in the minority in journalism, but they are a far from negligible force. Some statistics, at least in developed countries, would seem to indicate that the profession is now opening its doors wider to women than in the past. Does this mean there is no discrimination towards them?

Generally speaking, there is a kind of veiled discrimination in the working world. It takes the form of a definite concentration of women in certain professions or in those sectors of employment to which women gravitate, not as the result of any precise motives for choosing them or of any barriers raised against them in other activities, but through prejudice, tradition or apathy which set up fixed patterns and discourage new approaches. Journalism is no exception to this, since women are to be found in greater numbers in certain types of publication or in certain functions. As to their position in the hierarchy, there are unfortunately no general statistics. All that can be said from the scattered and limited information available is that women are not represented at the highest job levels in proportion to their total numbers or to the overall number of journalists.

In Japan, the Federation of Workers in Private Radio Stations states that, in certain companies, women do not enjoy equal opportunity in matters of recruitment, assignment, advancement and promotion. In the United Kingdom, in the daily press, women rarely rise to the rank of chief sub-editor; there are a few female editors in the provinces, but none in Fleet Street. More are to be found in the magazine press.[14] Women are not adequately represented in Canada, and are under-represented in the United States, except at lower levels of the hierarchy on "women's" columns or "practical living" columns. The higher posts are closed to them. In the United States, their position is less favourable in the radio and television news services than in the printed press. Most of them occupy inferior positions in which their function is to edit rather than to present the news and they are often given what are felt to be easy subjects to handle.[15]

Profession: Journalist

And yet the growth in the number of women working in many professions should also be evident in journalism. In fact, it has already begun. In France, the total number of departmental heads holding journalists' cards included 4 per cent of women in 1964 but rose to 23 per cent in the period from 1964 to 1971; the corresponding figures for editors were 10 and 13 per cent.[16] The special clauses contained in some of the collective agreements for the profession should accelerate this evolution. In New Zealand, where no woman has ever held the post of editor on a daily newspaper, it is to be assumed that the new legislation on equality of opportunity and pay should improve women's career chances in journalism; already, on some newspapers half of the reporters and several of the sub-editors are women.

Notes

[1] In France, the Identity Card Committee for Professional Journalists, referred to in Chapter 1, verifies the status of journalist but does not grant it. It is possible to practise the profession without a professional card.

[2] *West Africa*, op. cit., p. 433.

[3] Royal Commission on the Press: *Final report. Appendices*, p. 145.

[4] "L'agence France-Presse", in *Notes et études documentaires* (Paris, La documentation française), Nos. 4336-4337, 23 Nov. 1976, p. 52. The *grandes écoles* are colleges of university level specialising in professional teaching, e.g. the Ecole Polytechnique, Ecole des Arts et Métiers, etc.

[5] See the section on the conscience clause in Chapter 4.

[6] *Bericht der Bundesregierung über die Lage von Presse und Rundfunk in der Bundesrepublik Deutschland (1978)*, op. cit., p. 118.

[7] See Radi Vassilev: *La condition sociale des journalistes: Enquête comparative internationale — I* (Budapest, Interpress, 1976), pp. 55-56.

[8] ibid., p. 55.

[9] ACAS, op. cit., p. 163.

[10] Vassilev, op. cit., p. 56.

[11] "Afanasyev reports to journalists' congress", in *Current Digest of the Soviet Press* (Columbus, Ohio), 1977, No. 16, pp. 10-11.

[12] Vassilev, op. cit., pp. 58-59.

[13] *Le Monde* (Paris), 19 June 1980, p. 27.

[14] Central Youth Employment Executive, op. cit., pp. 36-37.

[15] UNESCO: *News media: Image, role and social conditions of women*, Studies and Information Documents, No. 84 (Paris, 1979), pp. 56 ff.

[16] CEREQ, op. cit., p. 68.

WEEKLY HOURS OF WORK, TIME OFF PER WEEK AND ANNUAL PAID LEAVE   6

The title of this chapter is as much of a surprise when related to journalists as it is when applied to many other categories of professional workers. Do writers, people engaged in scientific research or musicians really stop working when they put their pens or instruments down? Consciously or not, do they not continue to be obsessed by the theme of their work or research or by the piece they have just performed? Should they shut themselves off from all sources of inspiration for two days a week?

It is hard to imagine a reporter in search of a current news story being subjected to a fixed timetable, unless it were to be that of trains or aircraft. And what can be said of the political commentator or the drama critic? "At what moment can we catch him in the full swing of professional activity? Is it at the editorial offices of the paper, to which he will go, perhaps, to write or to dictate his article or simply to get into touch with his colleagues and to seek the latest news? Is it at the theatre, at a political meeting, or at home reading a critical work or a historical study, or yet again during his meal or during conversation with friends, when an idea flashes through his mind, bringing other ideas in its train and allowing him to build up, there and then, the entire framework of his article... Could he himself differentiate exactly between the moments devoted to his professional work and those reserved to undisturbed relaxation?" [1] These questions were framed more than 50 years ago but still remain as topical as ever, and it is still just as difficult to draw the line between the time a journalist spends on strictly professional activities and that which in other sectors is called rest time.

WEEKLY HOURS OF WORK

Certain regulations on the working conditions for journalists recognise these difficulties. Thus, in Switzerland, the decree of 14 January 1966 concerning the implementation of the federal law of 13 March 1964 on Work in Industry, Handicrafts and Commerce exempts the editorial staffs of newspapers and periodicals from some of its clauses concerning hours of work. It specifies that the employer can change the daily hours of work fixed by the basic law without official authorisation, but stipulates that work must not begin before 3 a.m. or go on beyond midnight and that there must be a daily rest period of ten consecutive hours (the latest collective agreement in French-speaking Switzerland increases this to 12 hours for day work and 14 for night work). The employer can also order work at night and on Sundays without official authorisation.

In some agreements, the question of hours of work has not been clearly codified. For example, the working code in Costa Rica classifies journalists as "trusted workers", subject to being available 12 hours a day. However, this does not mean that the normal day's work is as long as this. The national collective agreement in Tunisia on press enterprises states in article 15 that the parties recognise that the inherent requirements of the profession rule out the possibility of determining and dividing up the number of working hours, but that the parties will agree through internal arrangements in each enterprise on realistic conditions for compensation for hours of work in excess of the legal number. The national collective agreements in France and Italy deal with the matter in a similar way, except that in Italy the maximum weekly hours of work laid down by the agreement are substantially below the legal normal level: 36 hours instead of 48. This distinct difference clearly shows that, in the minds of the negotiating parties, the figure they have fixed is only a kind of "hard core" which allows for extra working hours, at least for certain categories of journalists, depending on working requirements. Certain jobs, such as those performed by news editors, sub-editors or news agency writers, must inevitably be carried out in the offices of the company and, consequently, are more easily measurable in terms of time; other jobs cannot be limited in time and space. It can also be assumed that, in many instances, the persons involved consider the number of hours fixed by law or contract only as a point of reference rather than as an inflexible rule.

Other documents regulate the number of hours of work in great detail and seem to be better suited to routine office work than to the ups and downs of journalistic work. The study published by the ILO in 1928 noted how minutely this question was codified in Australia. It still is, although perhaps to a lesser degree, as is suggested by the findings of an arbitration tribunal in 1974 concerning journalists on daily newspapers: the findings spell out what is to be understood by day work and night work, the breaks to be taken in both cases and naturally the normal daily working hours by day and by night, as well as working schedules during the Christmas period, Good Friday, etc.

Weekly hours of work

The frequency of a newspaper's publication obviously has an influence on hours of work and how they are divided. The production of an evening newspaper begins in the early hours of the morning; a morning newspaper starts production on the afternoon of the day before and continues until late at night. News agencies operate continuously and thus teams have to be organised and rotated. Normally, night shifts are shorter than day shifts. The result is that hours of work are often calculated on the basis of a period longer than one week. For example, the collective agreement for the provincial press in the United Kingdom stipulates that working hours must not exceed 80 hours in two consecutive weeks, excluding meal times, it being understood that journalists may be required to work some of these hours between 8 p.m. and 6 a.m., or at weekends.

In India, the limit is 144 hours, excluding meal times, for any four consecutive weeks; a journalist may not work for more than four consecutive hours on the day shift without taking one hour of rest, or for more than three-and-a-half hours on the night shift without a break of one-and-a-half hours. In Japan, one of the major daily newspapers has adopted seven hours a day as an average (including a one-hour break) and an average of 42 hours per week over four weeks; another has adopted eight hours and 48 hours; a television network has fixed 86 working hours over two weeks, with ten hours' break; and other daily newspapers and television stations calculate on a one-week basis. But the management of all these sections of the press agree that the actual working hours are between 50 and 60 per week.

The above statement seems to confirm the tendency, already noted, towards a discrepancy between normal hours of work and actual hours of work. In principle, and in so far as it can be calculated, the discrepancy is counterbalanced by extra pay for overtime and for other special circumstances (night work, weekend work, legal holidays), as will be seen later. The fact remains, however, that the fixing of normal hours of work is designed to meet the need of journalists for a legal or contractual form of protection rather than to limit the time they devote to their craft.

TIME OFF PER WEEK

Similar remarks could be made on the question of weekly breaks. Legislation and practice are tending to extend the breaks for all workers, and an increasing number now have two consecutive days off per week. It would be unjust for journalists to be isolated from this social development. But the character and demands of their profession represent a major obstacle, by virtue of the fact that the dividing line between work and leisure time is hard to draw and that work requirements often encroach on normal weekends off. In particular, Monday morning newspapers are made up on Sunday, radio and television stations issue news programmes during weekends as well as on other days, and sports reporters are at their busiest when most of the public is relaxing.

This explains why the rules on weekly leave for journalists are different from the general norms. The Weekly Rest (Commerce and Offices) Convention (No. 106), adopted by the International Labour Conference in 1957, includes press enterprises among the categories to which States may declare this instrument to be applicable, which, conversely, means that they may be excluded from its application. As the Convention provides for the possibility of special arrangements a number of different situations are to be found. Legislative measures in some countries are silent on the question so far as journalists are concerned (Federal Republic of Germany), or simply refer to the principle of weekly rest without defining its length or conditions (Argentina). Others contain special measures for journalists. For instance, the Swiss decree of 1966, mentioned earlier in connection with working hours, exempts the press employer from requesting official authorisation for making staff work on a Sunday; it states that when Sunday work extends into the morning or afternoon, and lasts more than five hours, it must be compensated for, either in the preceding or the following week by at least 24 hours' consecutive leave on a working day; sports journalists must have at least one entire Sunday free and other journalists at least two Sundays every four weeks. In Poland, the journalist has the right to one day off per week which must be on a Sunday at least once in every three weeks.

Collective agreements, decisions by arbitrators and regulations in companies supplement the silence of the law on this matter, or bring about improvements in its measures. They may limit themselves, as is the case with the collective agreements concerning the major press news agencies in the United States, to laying down the principle of a five-day working week, consecutive or not, which would suggest two days off per week. These would not necessarily be the normal weekend, and the two days could be split. In Canada, the collective agreements establish a five-day week; some specify that it must be consecutive, others are silent on the matter; the result is that there are two days off, but on some newspapers these are split; work on Sundays is allowed. The decision by the tribunal in Australia, mentioned above, makes a distinction between night and day work. In Japan, weekly leave is one day on daily newspapers, with the possibility of spreading the four days over four weeks; magazines and certain television networks grant more leave, sometimes two days per week. By the terms of the collective agreement for the provincial press in the United Kingdom, journalists normally have the right to eight days' leave every four consecutive weeks, which must include at least two periods of two consecutive days; under this plan, every effort is made to let them have Sundays free, if service requirements so allow; if not, Sunday work is done on a rotating system.

Weekly hours of work

Thus, the extension of the basis of calculation beyond one week and the rotation of Sunday work are two methods which can be used to reconcile two conflicting aims: the appearance of the newspaper to meet public demand, and the granting of reasonable weekly time off, including the traditional weekend where possible.

Table 6 shows the normal hours of work and weekly leave for journalists in 57 countries. The table would suggest that, in theory, journalists enjoy the same rights in this area as most other workers, and even greater rights in some countries. But, for a more accurate picture of the situation, it should not be overlooked that the figures refer to normal hours of work, or, to quote the terms of the Reduction of Hours of Work Recommendation, 1962 (No. 116), "the number of hours fixed in each country or in pursuance of laws or regulations, collective agreements or arbitration awards, or, where not so fixed, the number of hours in excess of which any time worked is remunerated at overtime rates or forms an exception to the recognised rules or custom of the establishment or of the process concerned". It is evident that the nature of a journalist's work means that actual working hours are quite different from normal ones.

According to the Union of Journalists in the Federal Republic of Germany, weekly working hours for the editorial staffs of dailies were between 30 and 60 in 1978, whereas magazine staffs in general had a 40-hour working week. The normal working schedule laid down by agreement was 195 hours per month (45 hours per week). In Costa Rica, the practice is seven hours a day on a five-day week basis, plus a few hours on Saturdays and legal holidays, a working week shorter than that laid down by law which is 48 hours. In Spain, the normal working day is six hours, but can go up to eight hours. In Hong Kong it is eight hours a day, but in practice it is usually between five and eight hours. In Iraq, it can be as much as 12 hours a day, the normal time being six hours. In Japan, the actual working day is longer than the normal one. In Madagascar, journalists work from ten to 12 hours a day. In New Zealand, where the normal working week is 40 hours, the actual number is 7 per cent higher on average. In Senegal, the legal norm is 40 hours a week, but journalists are obliged to work abnormal hours and also during legal holidays and are therefore paid on the basis of a 48-hour week.

Some collective agreements specify not only the number of hours of work but also when the working day should begin and end. In Canada, this varies between eight and eight-and-a-half consecutive hours, depending on the company; by agreement, sports writers and theatre critics are exceptions to this rule. In Italy, the day's work must not exceed ten consecutive hours.

An interesting feature of the profession in Bulgaria is that journalists can be granted a daily credit of two hours for creative work: for those

Profession: Journalist

Table 6. Normal hours of work and time off per week

Country	Normal hours of work	Time off per week
Argentina	36 h per week	48 h according to certain collective agreements
Australia	40 h per week for day work 38 h per week for night work	48 h consecutively
Austria	42 h per week	1 to 2 days depending on the undertaking
Barbados	8 h per day and 40 h per week	2 days
Belgium	38 h per week	2 days
Brazil	5 h per day (possibly + 2 h in addition)	1 day
Bulgaria	8 h daily for day work 6 h daily for night work	38 h
United Republic of Cameroon	40 h per week (5 days of 7 h and 1 day of 5 h)	1 day (Saturday or Sunday)
Canada	35 to $37^1/_2$ (according to the undertaking) in 5 days	2 days
Chile	48 h in 6 days	1 day
Congo	40 h per week	
Costa Rica	48 h per week	1 day
Cuba	44 h per week	
Czechoslovakia	$42^1/_2$ in 5 days	2 days
Denmark	40 h per week	
Ecuador	44 h per week	No rule
Egypt	46 h per week	1 day
Ethiopia		$1^1/_2$ days
Finland	$37^1/_2$ h in 4 or 5 days	2 days
France	39 h per week	2 days
German Democratic Republic	$43^3/_4$ h in 5 days	2 days
Federal Republic of Germany	195 h per month [1] $42^1/_2$ to 43 h per week (radio and television)	2 days
Ghana	8 h per day	2 days
Greece	30 h in 5 days	2 days
Guyana	40 h in 6 days	1 day
Honduras	8 h daily and 44 h per week for day work 6 h daily and 36 h per week for night work	1 day
Hong Kong	8 h per day	1 day
Hungary	42 to 46 h per week	1 or 2 days
Iceland	40 h per week	
India	144 h in 4 weeks	24 h
Iraq	6 h daily	1 day
Ireland	35 h or 36 h per week	2 days
Italy	36 h in 5 days	2 days

Weekly hours of work

Table 6. *(continued)*

Country	Normal hours of work	Time off per week
Japan	7 to 8 h per day 42 to 48 h per week (depending on the undertaking)	1 or more days (depending on the undertaking)
Jordan	48 h in 6 days	1 day
Kuwait		1 day
Libyan Arab Jamahiriya	8 h per day	1 day
Madagascar		1½ days
Malaysia	6 to 8 h per day (depending on the team)	1 to 2 days (depending on the undertaking)
Netherlands	40 h per week	
New Zealand	40 h in 5 days	2 days
Norway	42 h per week	
Pakistan	42 h per week	1 day
Philippines	8 h per day	
Poland	42 h per week	1 day
Senegal	40 h per week	
Sierra Leone	45 h per week	
Spain	6 h per day 5 days per week (with rotation for the 6th)	2 days
Sri Lanka	43 h per week	1½ days
Sweden	40 h per week	36 h
Switzerland	Regulations concerning starting and finishing times and for daily rest time	1½ days for day work 2 days for night work
Tunisia	40 h per week	24 h
Turkey	42 h	
USSR	41 h in 5 or 6 days	42 h
United Kingdom	80 h per 2 weeks (day work) 70 h per 2 weeks (night work)	8 days in 4 weeks
United States	33¾ to 40 h per week depending on the company and grade (most common is 37½ h)	1½ days
Uruguay	36 h	

[1] A reduction to 40 hours per week will be introduced progressively from 1 January 1984.

Sources. Replies to ILO questionnaire, legislation, arbitration awards, collective agreements, International Federation of Journalists, International Organisation of Journalists.

who benefit from this, obligatory working hours in the news-room are cut down from 42 to 32 in a working week of five days (usual practice) and from 46 to 34 in a six-day working week.

* * *

As can be seen, hours of work for journalists are subject to a great deal of variation. Only an incomplete idea of the differences between the various information media — daily newspapers, magazines, news agencies, radio and television stations — has been given above. The two international organisations for journalists are also constantly concerned with the establishment in all countries of a 40-hour,[2] five-day working week with two days off. They thus hope to help journalists, in those countries still untouched by it, to benefit from the general movement now spreading to all sectors of activity towards a reduction not only of normal hours of work but also of actual hours of work.

ANNUAL PAID LEAVE

The concept of weekly working hours and time off may not always have the same meaning for journalists as for other workers, but where "paid leave" is concerned, they are not at a disadvantage. On the contrary, journalists are favoured in this respect by comparison with the average worker, as if to provide them with compensation for the rigorous demands of their normal working hours. In any case, the holiday season, at least on the national level, is usually a slack period from the news point of view: there are fewer political and social events and the reduced size of newspapers and radio and television news bulletins reflects the annual slowdown in national life as the public flocks to holiday resorts.

In a similar fashion to many other sectors of activity, the length of annual paid leave for journalists depends on a whole range of legislative and contractual arrangements — collective or individual. Table 7 gives some idea of the extent of this diversity. It shows that, in the 53 countries covered, paid annual leave can range from two weeks to one-and-a-half months and even more in extreme cases. But the picture is incomplete for two reasons.

The first is that, while the legal duration of leave is common knowledge and easy to determine in a given country, since it is laid down in collective agreements, the nature of individual contracts and of unofficial individual arrangements made on a non-contractual basis is generally not known by third parties.

The other reason is that the number of legal holidays has to be taken into account. They do not fall under the definition of annual holidays as such, but are still free days officially recognised and paid for which, in fact, shorten the annual amount of time spent at work — a concept which is now being used more and more in international comparisons.

Table 7. Annual paid leave

Argentina	15 working days for less than 10 years of service 20 working days for 10 to 20 years of service 30 working days for more than 20 years of service plus 3, 5 or 7 days, respectively, if the work is normally performed at night
Australia	6 weeks
Austria	26 working days 39 working days after 10 years of service
Belgium	25 to 30 days depending on number of years of service
Brazil	30 days
Bulgaria	20 to 30 working days according to duties and number of years of service
United Republic of Cameroon	Civil servants: 1 month Others: $1^1/_2$ working days per month of service plus 2 working days per year for every 5 years of service
Canada	3 to 5 weeks according to the number of years of service
Chile	15 working days (25 in some regions) plus 1 day for every 3 years after 10 years of service; maximum 30 days
Costa Rica	2 weeks
Cuba	1 month
Czechoslovakia	2 weeks during the first 5 years of service 3 weeks after 5 years of service 4 weeks after 15 years of service
Denmark	Provincial press: 6 weeks National press: 7 weeks
Ecuador	15 days, plus 1 day for each year of service in the company
Egypt	30 to 45 days according to number of years of service and membership of a union
Finland	5 to 7 weeks according to grade and number of years of service
France	1 month after 1 year in the company plus 1 week after 8 years in the company and in the profession (more in certain companies)
German Democratic Republic	21 to 32 working days according to number of years of service
Federal Republic of Germany	25 days for 1 to 5 years of service 28 days for 6 to 7 years of service 30 days for 8 to 19 years of service 34 days for 20 years or more of service and from the age of 45
Ghana	21 to 30 working days according to number of years of service
Greece	30 days
Guyana	3 weeks per year, 2 months every 4 years
Honduras	10 working days after 1 year of service 12 working days after 2 years of service 15 working days after 3 years of service 20 working days after 4 years of service
Hong Kong	Minimum of 7 days after 12 months of continuous service in the same company (extra leave depending on individual contracts)
Hungary	12 to 24 working days according to function and number of years of service

Profession: Journalist

Table 7. *(continued)*

Iceland	24 working days
	27 working days after 5 years of service
India	One-eleventh of the duration of service for the year
Iraq	36 days
Ireland	6 weeks
Italy	26 working days up to 5 years of service
	30 working days for 5 to 15 years of service
	35 working days after 15 years of service
	Plus 5 days of "leave" after 1 year of service in the company
Japan	*(See text)*
Jordan	3 weeks
Libyan Arab Jamahiriya	(The same as for public servants)
Madagascar	30 days
Malaysia	Apprentices: 14 working days
	Licensed journalists up to 18 years of service: 21 working days
	Licensed journalists after 18 years of service: 24 working days
Mongolia	26 working days
Netherlands	$4^1/_2$ weeks
	Plus supplement depending on age
New Zealand	4 weeks
	Plus 1 week after 10 years in the company
Norway	4 weeks
	5 weeks after 10 years in the profession
	6 weeks after 60 years of age
Pakistan	Minimum of one-eleventh of the length of service during the year
Philippines	15 days
Poland	(a) According to the Labour Code:
	14 working days after 1 year of service
	17 working days after 3 years of service
	20 working days after 6 years of service
	26 working days after 10 years of service
	(b) According to the national collective agreement: supplement of 12 days after 15 years in the profession
Senegal	1 month
Sierra Leone	3 weeks for senior journalists
	2 weeks for others
Spain	30 days
Sweden	25 days if under 40 years of age
	30 days after 40 years of age
	For radio journalists: similar leave with a supplement of 3 to 5 days for those above certain salary scales
Switzerland	4 weeks up to 40 years of age
	5 weeks after 40 years of age
	6 weeks after 50 years of age
	1 extra week for news editors doing 4 night shifts (i.e., 3 hours or more of work between 7 p.m. and 7 a.m.) per week
Tunisia	1 month after 1 year of service
	5 weeks after 10 years in the profession

Weekly hours of work

Table 7. *(continued)*

Turkey	1 month
	45 days after 10 years of service
USSR	24 working days (up to 42 working days in the Far North)
United Kingdom	5 weeks for senior journalists
	3 weeks for junior journalists
	4 weeks for others
United States	2 weeks minimum, but normally 3 weeks, plus extra leave according to number of years of service up to a total leave of 4 to 5 weeks in most companies
Uruguay	20 working days, plus 1 working day for every 4 years in the same company after the first 5 years

Sources. Replies to ILO questionnaire, legislation, arbitration awards, collective agreements, International Federation of Journalists, International Organisation of Journalists.

The number of legal holidays varies considerably from one country to another, from one state or province to another inside the same country (Federal Republic of Germany), or even from one company to another (Canada, Japan, United States). The collective agreement for Italian journalists is a sign of the importance given by the profession to national and religious traditions in this respect: a law passed in 1977 abolished seven of the 17 legal holidays which were previously recognised. However, the collective agreement stipulates (article 19) that work on these seven days must be paid at special rates, on the basis of one twenty-sixth of the monthly salary, increased by 80 per cent.

The disparities in the situation are naturally accentuated by the different elements to be taken into account in fixing the duration of annual leave: the length of service in the profession and in the enterprise, the age of the journalist and the amount of service in the year under consideration. The result is that the rules are very different from one country to another and from one enterprise to the next.

In this context, the situation in Japan is of especial interest. For example, one of the major dailies in this country grants 25 days of annual paid leave to employees with 18 months or more of service or to those who have worked 80 per cent or more working days between 1 April of the preceding year and 31 March of the year under consideration, but only 13 days to those who have worked 50 to 79 per cent of the working days in the same period. For those with less than 18 months' service, leave is granted according to the date when they were engaged: those with "almost" 18 months' service are granted 23 days' leave if they have worked 80 per cent or more working days between the starting date of their service and 31 March of the year under consideration, and 13 days if they have worked 50 to 70 per cent working days. Those with nearly one year's service and who have worked 80 per cent or more working days since their starting date receive 11 to 13 days' leave. It will be noted that the legal minimum is only six days.

Profession: Journalist

The rules are as follows at another Japanese daily newspaper:

Length of service (as of 1 December)	Days of paid leave	
	Having worked 90 per cent or more working days	Having worked 80 to 90 per cent working days
1-4 years	20	18
5-9 years	25	22
10 years or more	30	27

If the duration of service is less than one year but more than six months, the leave is as follows:

Months of service	Days of paid leave
6	10
7	11
8	12
9	13
10	14
11	15

In all cases, 12 national legal holidays are added.

Magazines and television stations in Japan each have their own leave scales which differ from those given in the tables.

Thus, journalists in this country are subjected to various systems which, however, have one point in common: the importance given to length of service in the company, a powerful incentive to loyalty to the publication. This is also a marked feature in many other countries, as can be seen from table 7 (Argentina, Canada, Finland, Honduras, Italy, Poland, United States).

Other characteristics should also be noted:

— extra leave for night work (Argentina, Switzerland);
— duties (Bulgaria, Hungary) or membership of the trade union (Egypt);
— advantages given to the national press over the provincial press (Denmark);
— consideration given to training periods in calculating years of service (Poland);
— application of more favourable terms by reason of the severity of living conditions (USSR).

As with their action on weekly working hours and reduction of time at work, the two international organisations for journalists have formulated similar objectives. The IFJ believes that the minimum amount of paid leave should be five weeks a year with a supplement for length of service. The IOJ recommends a minimum of 26 working days with more for length of service — apart from such questions as age and duties or membership of unions; in addition, the IOJ feels that the overall number of years at work, not just in the profession or the enterprise, should be taken into account at the rate of one working day for each year of service.

To complete the picture, it should be noted that "special leave" is granted to journalists in certain personal or family circumstances, usually through the application of collective agreements. Examples of such leave for journalists are:

— in France, six days for their marriage, two days for the marriage of a child or for moving house, three days for the birth of a child, from one to four days for the death of a close relative;
— in the Federal Republic of Germany, two or three days for moving house, two days for their marriage, the birth of a child or death of a close relative;
— in New Zealand, three days for the death of a marriage partner, a child or relative, one day for the death of a brother, sister or parent-in-law;
— in Senegal, three days for their marriage, one day for the birth and two days for the baptism of a child, one day for the marriage of a close relative and one or two days for the death of a close relative, all up to a maximum of ten days a year;
— in Tunisia, two days for their marriage, one day for the birth of a child, one or two days for the death of a close relative.

Notes

[1] ILO: *Conditions of work and life of journalists*, op. cit., pp. 100-101.
[2] According to the International Federation of Journalists, 35 hours for night work.

PAY   7

The salary costs in a press undertaking, including those of journalists, represent a substantial proportion of the total sales price. In the United Kingdom, in 1975, the percentage costs for production and editorial staff on daily newspapers were respectively as follows: national "quality" newspapers, 31 and 17 per cent; national "popular" newspapers, 30 and 13 per cent; provincial "quality" newspapers, 32 and 13 per cent; provincial "popular" newspapers, 31 and 11 per cent.[1] In the same period, it was estimated in France that editorial expenses represented an average of 20 per cent of the selling price of a newspaper.[2] These are far from negligible figures and it is easy to understand that newspaper managements try to control overall salaries, in particular by seeking to avoid double employment of printing and editorial staff — a possible sequel to the introduction of the new technology, and especially to the use of computers and photocomposition machines. The distribution of costs has undergone certain changes in recent years: the amortisation of new equipment and particularly the sharp rise in newsprint have considerably increased costs for materials, and staff expenses — particularly those for printing staff, who are more affected than others by modern methods — have somewhat receded in importance. The fact remains that, for journalists and printers, the question of pay is of prime importance.

As is the case in most professions, pay for journalists is composed of a number of elements which can be split into two categories: basic salary and a whole range of bonuses and compensation payments. These component parts are established by the State (law or decree in Argentina or Chile for example), by governmental authority in consultation with representatives of the interested parties (Costa Rica, USSR), by collective bargaining (in most countries) on the national, provincial or local level, or with the enterprise, by direct and individual agreement, written or simply verbal (Honduras), or by a combination of several of these methods.

Profession: Journalist

BASIC SALARY

Regardless of how it is determined — with the exception of certain individual agreements — the basic pay is fixed in relation to a salary scale in which each level usually represents the minimum payable for a specific job or group of jobs or, in certain cases, a spread between the minimum and maximum. These scales are somewhat complex, as can be seen from the following examples.

In Australia, according to the arbitration awards mentioned earlier, a different minimum salary is applicable to the six grades into which journalists in each company are divided in a fixed proportion. The proportions from top to bottom are as follows: Grade A special and A2, 10 per cent each of the total staff; grade A, 15 per cent; grade B, 35 per cent; grades C and D, 15 per cent each.

In Canada, one collective agreement recognises 19 minimum salary levels for editorial staff, depending on their function, but only eight concern journalists as such. In some cases, the minimum varies according to length of service: six grades, based on length of service, are laid down for reporters. Other agreements class journalists in four or five groups, with length of service also being taken into account for fixing a minimum wage for the lower groups, but only for a few years.

In France, the scales fixed by collective agreements consist of up to 30 levels, each corresponding to a hierarchical coefficient and to one or several jobs; the scales are determined jointly for all types of press publications, by agreement between employers' and journalists' organisations. There are separate scales for Paris dailies, regional dailies, local dailies, weeklies, other periodicals, radio and television, news agencies, etc. Pay varies in certain cases, depending on the category. Paris weeklies are classified into three categories, depending on whether their circulation is above 100,000 copies, from 40,000 to 100,000, or fewer than 40,000 copies. Other Paris publications are also classified into three categories: the first covers those which deal with all major news items and politics and which are aimed at the public in general; the second category also covers publications aimed at the general public but with a definite specialisation and approach; the third covers those designed for a more restricted public, particularly publications of technical or specialist interest. The situation is made more complex by the fact that the same qualification does not correspond to the same hierarchical coefficient in the various sections of the press. A chief editor has a coefficient of 333 in the Paris dailies and in Agence France-Press, 300 on the regional dailies, 250 at Radio-France and 230 on the local dailies. Certain scales, but not all, fix the pay for freelance journalists and illustrators. An interesting feature is the annual establishment by the Government of a list of companies which contract to pay their journalists, for the year in question, a salary not less than those fixed, for each professional category and each department or region, by a joint commission of representatives of professional organisations of newspaper and magazine directors or publishers and journalists' organisations.[3]

In India, salary scales are fixed in the same way: newspapers are classified into nine categories, based on their annual gross revenue and not on circulation, and journalists are divided into four main groups. As noted in the Introduction, rates are fixed by a Wage Board: set up by the central Government, this Board consists of two employers' representatives, two journalists' representatives and three independent persons of whom one is, or has been, a High Court or Supreme Court judge; the latter acts as chairman of the council. In 1979, because this Board did not function effectively, the Government created a tribunal, headed by an acting or former judge of the High Court or Supreme Court and empowered to establish or revise salary scales.[4]

In Iraq, the law on practising the profession of journalism includes a scale of salaries which sets out the limits for different jobs. Diplomas and length of service are taken into account.

The collective agreement for the Italian press distinguishes four categories of journalists for the purpose of fixing minimum salaries: reporters with less than 18 months of professional service, other reporters, news editors in news-rooms with more than five reporters, and chief editors.

The Japanese press is a good example of the complexity involved in calculating a basic salary. In most cases, this is mainly based — true to Japanese tradition — on age, level of education and length of service, although in certain companies it also depends on the nature of the job and on the ability of the persons concerned — elements which are becoming increasingly important. To take one of the leading newspapers as an example, the basic salary is made up as follows: *(a)* payment for ability which varies depending on educational level; *(b)* payment according to age which increases from 16 to 50 years of age, after which it remains fixed; *(c)* payment for length of service which is calculated by multiplying a basic amount by the number of years of service. The following formula, used by a magazine, does not take ability into account:

Basic salary in Yen:

$$131{,}400 + 4{,}500\,(N\text{-}22) + 60\,(40x\text{-}x^2) + 2{,}350K + 15\,(33K\text{-}K^2)$$

where
N = age at date of application of the formula
$x = N\text{-}20$
K = length of service in the company or other companies at the same date

The formula does not apply under the age of 20, or when the binomial $(33K\text{-}K^2)$ is negative.

In the United Kingdom, minimum salary scales are traditionally negotiated at the national level for the national press and for the provincial press. They are drawn up on the basis of the minimum rate for a professional journalist, that is, one who has reached the age of 24 and is thus considered fully trained and qualified. But, in practice, while using these national scales, individual press companies establish their own scales with the unions concerned, the structure and levels of which vary from one to another. For example, the agreement of 1978 for the provincial press provided for no less than 18 minimum rates for fully qualified journalists, plus a certain number of minimum rates for journalists in training, calculated in percentages of the full rates. A provincial newspaper recognises only seven grades: trainees, newly qualified journalists, those with two years or more of continuous service in journalism in the United Kingdom, those with the same length of service in the company, those with five years of general experience in the profession, those with five years of continuous service in the company, and, finally, those who perform functions considered by the chief editor as carrying special responsibilities. The salary scale at Reuters news agency has a dozen grades. It should be added that these minimum rates vary according to the category of the newspaper which itself depends on its frequency of publication, its coverage and circulation. There are six groups in the provincial press. Naturally, press undertakings are at liberty to grant individual journalists higher rates of pay, not to mention "merit payments" which will be referred to later. The result is that pay scales for journalists in the United Kingdom are as diversified and impenetrable as can be found anywhere.

In Sweden, the minimum salary scales are fixed by collective agreement and are based on length of service. They consist of six levels and correspond to the first job and to one, three, six, nine and 15 years of service in the profession. Similarly, the Swiss collective agreement sets up minimum salary levels which go up with the number of years a journalist has been entered on the professional register and actual salaries are worked out through individual arrangements.

In Tunisia, under the national agreement, the scale of salaries covers several categories based on the hierarchy: performance of the job, limited or complete mastery of the profession, executive responsibility and senior executive responsibility; the jobs, from archives to chief editor, are spread over these categories. Within each category, salaries go up by length of service. A joint commission, similar to that in France, fixes minimum salaries for each category and each region. The same kind of system operates in Senegal.

Basic salary scales for journalists are also applied in the socialist countries.[5] In some of them, it is the central authority which establishes these scales, in co-operation with the unions: in Bulgaria, it is the Council of Ministers; in Czechoslovakia, the Ministry of Labour and Social

Affairs; and in the USSR, the Council of Ministers or the State Committee for Labour and Social Questions. Elsewhere, the scales are fixed through collective agreements: Cuba, the German Democratic Republic, Hungary and Poland. In some of these countries — Bulgaria, Hungary, the USSR — they vary according to the importance and category of the press undertaking: newspapers, reviews, news agencies, radio or television, national, regional or local newspapers, general or specialised news, etc. Based on information provided by the Government in Poland, the national collective agreement distinguishes 20 functions or groups of functions, ranging from trainee to editor. In this country, journalists are expected to produce a volume of work corresponding to a "norm" in return for the basic salary in their group. For work over the norm, they receive extra payment; this norm is not applicable to certain functions — for example, the editor or chief sub-editor; older journalists are also partially or totally exempted.

COMPENSATION FOR OVERTIME

The frequency of publication of a newspaper is a determining factor in both working hours and how they are apportioned. Newspapers and periodicals appear at fixed hours and on precise dates. The result is that journalists work at times which can be described as "abnormal" or "atypical" or, when incompatible with normal family and social life, "anti-social". Such working schedules are probably less arduous in general than those in certain industrial sectors where the need to meet production targets keeps workers under constant pressure. However, the major news agencies work on a 24-hour basis, and the production of morning dailies requires the presence of journalists late at night and during the traditional weekly rest day (called "Sunday" here for simplification, although it is Friday or Saturday in many countries).

It is clear that, in choosing this profession, every journalist accepts in advance the handicaps that go with it, including erratic working hours. In fact, the rules in the profession leave no doubt on this. Thus the national collective agreement for the French press indicates that the parties recognise that the inherent needs of the profession rule out the question of allocating working hours (article 26). The same text, while laying down the principles of compensation for night work, excludes certain categories, for example reporters who do not qualify as regular night workers, columnists, theatre critics whose function is by definition to work in the evening (article 27), etc. In Austria, there is no provision for compensation for night work. In Poland, overtime and work on Sundays and legal holidays also give no entitlement to compensation. In Costa Rica, where being available for 12 hours a day is standard practice, all work done during this period is paid at normal rates.

Profession: Journalist

Table 8. Compensation for overtime, night work, Sunday work and work on public holidays

Country	Overtime	Night work	Sunday work (S) Work on legal holidays (H)
Argentina	Compensatory free time the next day or during the week or double pay (maximum: 20 hours per month)	Additional annual vacation of 3 to 7 days	Compensatory free time in the following week or double pay
Australia	+ 50 or 100% of hourly pay depending on the case	+ 10% from 6 to 7 a.m. and from 6 to 8.30 p.m. + 17.5% from 8.30 p.m. to 6 a.m.	+ 7.5%
Austria			+ 5% of monthly salary (S)
Belgium		Compensatory free time	Compensatory free time or $1/22$ of monthly salary (minimum: 4 hours' work)
Canada	Depending on the company: + 50% or free time in the 3 months, or + 50% for the 1st hour and + 100% thereafter	+ 7.5% in some companies	Double pay (only H in some companies)
Chile	+ 50%	Depends on the agreement between the parties	
Costa Rica			Double pay
Denmark		+ 5%	+ 7%
Finland		Lump sum bonus	Double pay (S)
France	Compensatory free time	+ 15% from 9 p.m. to 6 a.m. (if work ends after 11 p.m.)	Compensatory free time
Federal Republic of Germany	Equivalent free time in the following 2 months or a payment of $1/150$ of monthly salary	(No regulations for periodicals)	Additional pay after 4 hours or a free day in the following 4 weeks
Guyana	Free time or incentive bonuses	Free time or incentive bonuses	+ 100% (S) + 50% or 100% (H)
Honduras	+ 25% for day work + 50 to 75% for night work	+ 25%	Double pay, plus additional free time

Table 8. *(continued)*

Country	Overtime	Night work	Sunday work (S) Work on legal holidays (H)
Hong Kong			Compensatory free time (H)
India		Longer breaks between shifts	
Ireland	Compensatory free time	Compensatory free time	Compensatory free time
Italy	+ 20%	+ 16%	$1/20$ of monthly salary increased by 80% plus 1 day free if the legal holiday falls on a Sunday
Japan	Daily newspapers: monthly bonus paid as a lump sum Magazines and TV: varies from company to company		
Libyan Arab Jamahiriya	Senior executives: monthly bonus equivalent to $1/3$ of salary Other staff: variable hourly payment, doubled for work on normal free days and legal holidays		
New Zealand	+ 50% for the first 3 hours + 100% thereafter	Lump sum bonus	+ 50% for Saturday morning + 100% for Saturday afternoon and Sunday + 100% on legal holidays (minimum: 4 hours)
Norway		Lump sum bonus	Lump sum (S)
Pakistan	+ 100%	"Agreed" compensation	+ 100%
Philippines	+ 50%		+ 50% for the first 8 hours + 100% thereafter
Poland		Special additional payments	
Spain		+ 25%	$1^1/_2$ days' free time

Profession: Journalist

Table 8. *(continued)*

Country	Overtime	Night work	Sunday work (S) Work on legal holidays (H)
Sweden	*(See table in the text)*	Compensation according to a points system	Compensation according to a points system (S) Lump sum payment (H)
Switzerland	At least + 25%, or equivalent free time	Additional vacation allowance when night or Sunday work is carried out on a regular basis	
Tunisia	Depending on company rules	+ 15%	+ 100% (H)
Turkey			+ 50%
United Kingdom	Equivalent free time	Reduced working hours	
United States	+ 50%	+ 2.5 to 15%	Compensation equal to 100, 150 or 200%, depending on the company, in pay or free time (H)

Sources. Replies to ILO questionnaire, legislation, arbitration awards, collective agreements, International Federation of Journalists.

However, just as normal working hours have finally been regulated for journalists in many countries, as they have for most other categories of workers, so compensation for abnormal working hours is today subject to regulations. According to a study by the Newspaper Guild of 218 collective agreements negotiated by this union in the United States and Canada, and operative on 25 June 1975, 182 guaranteed extra pay for night work; these 182 contracts covered a total of 140 agreements with newspapers (166 newspapers in all), eight agreements with news agencies and 34 miscellaneous agreements.

Table 8 summarises the measures applicable in a certain number of countries for payment of overtime, work on Sundays, work at night and work on legal holidays. The table is an indication of the wide variety of solutions which have been devised, from compensation to the choice available in many cases between salary increases or additional leave. Less clear — due to the need to simplify the table — is the complexity of certain measures which have been adopted.

The rules governing the payment of overtime in Sweden, under the national collective agreement of 1978, are a good illustration of this complexity, due in this instance to the fact that the negotiating parties

Pay

wished to make a distinction between the different days of the week and various shifts. Compensation is made in two possible ways, depending on whether overtime involves cash payment or time off:

Additional hours	Cash: monthly salary divided by	Time off: number of overtime hours multiplied by
Weekdays (except Saturday)		
from 6 a.m. to 7 a.m.	100	1.75
from 7 a.m. to 6 p.m.	110	1.50
Weekdays (except Friday and Saturday)		
from 6 p.m. to 10 p.m.	100	1.75
Weekdays from 10 p.m. to 6 a.m.	85	2.00
From Friday 6 p.m. to Monday 6 a.m.		

In several countries, the burden of night work is recognised not by an increase in salary or additional leave, but by a reduction in the normal working hours or an extension of the normal rest periods. In the Philippines, a collective agreement establishes that overtime is valid after eight hours of work by day and only seven at night. In the United Kingdom, as shown in table 6, the normal working hours are 80 hours for two weeks' day work and 70 hours for two weeks' night work. In India, as previously mentioned, the law stipulates that journalists must not work more than four hours continuously by day, followed by one hour of rest, and three hours by night, followed by one-and-a-half hours of rest.

BONUSES AND ALLOWANCES

This component of pay is widely practised in the press world as in most salaried professions. There is probably no country where it does not exist in one form or another and it often represents a substantial portion of the total pay packet. It takes several forms, which can be broken down under four main headings: cost of living allowance; additional pay for long service; participation in profits and bonuses for performance and merit; compensation for professional expenses and other allowances.

Cost of living allowance

This is an aspect of pay which has become habitual and it is by no means confined to the profession of journalism. There is thus no need to dwell on it. It is simply worth noting that in certain countries adjustment to the cost of living is made automatically, whereas in others it is negotiated periodically or determined by the public authorities when deemed appropriate; sometimes the indemnity is incorporated in the salary and, in these cases, the adjustment is made after basic salary scales have been changed. In periods of high inflation, this can cause fluctuations in pay which affect journalists adversely.

Additional pay for long service

Long service in the company or profession is almost always rewarded by additional pay. It is often taken into account in the salary scales. As has been seen in the preceding pages, this is the case in Canada, Iraq, Italy, Japan, Sweden, Tunisia and the United Kingdom. The same applies to Austria, Egypt, Senegal, Spain, Switzerland, Uruguay and in the socialist countries. In some of the latter countries, additional pay for long service represents a particularly substantial addition.[6] In Bulgaria, for example, pay is increased by 4 per cent after five years of employment, 8 per cent after ten years, 12 per cent after 15 years and 16 per cent after 20 years. In Poland, as well as additional pay after five, ten and 15 years of service, journalists receive a single bonus equivalent to one month's salary after 20 years of service. At the end of five years of service, journalists in the German Democratic Republic receive a loyalty bonus, also equal to one month's salary, without prejudice to regular bonuses for long service.

Additional pay for long service in other countries is linked to salary scales, but is not incorporated in them. France has been cited as an example in Chapter 5. There, the combination of long service in both the profession and the enterprise ensures that journalists progress to a certain degree in their career, even without promotion. In other countries, such as Argentina, additional pay does not take the form of a salary percentage but of a lump sum which increases with the number of years of service up to a maximum of 20.[7]

A final group of countries should be noted — Jordan, for example [8] — where long service is not taken into account in calculating pay.

Participation in profits and performance or merit bonuses

In many countries, it has become the practice to pay salaried workers in the private sector, at fixed dates (middle or end of year), a sum equal to one or two months' salary, in addition to normal pay. This practice is frequently applied to journalists who thus receive a thirteenth, often a fourteenth and even a fifteenth monthly salary; in Japan, the total amount of these bonuses can be equal to as much as six to ten months' salary.

Should these payments be regarded as a participation in profits? Theoretically, yes. But in reality, the regularity of these payments, their mathematical relation to salary scales, and the fact that they are in the majority of cases paid regardless of the financial results of the company, would seem to contradict this assumption. What they really amount to is a supplementary salary paid once or several times a year instead of every month.

Some newspapers make a direct connection between these bonuses and their actual profits. For example, one company in Costa Rica distributes dividends among those employees who have a minimum of five years of service. In Pakistan, the legislation stipulates that all employees with more than three months of service during the year in question are entitled to their share of 30 per cent of the profits, provided that this share is less than their monthly salary. In the USSR, if the enterprise covers its costs without a state subsidy, journalists have their salary increased by 10 per cent. In New Zealand, certain newspapers have established a system of participation in profits, others a Christmas bonus — the amounts in both cases being at the discretion of the employer. Others have nothing of this kind.

Whether independent of, or based on, the newspaper's financial results, most of these salary supplements benefit all those who work on the newspaper. There are other forms of bonus payments which are linked to individual work: these are performance or merit bonuses.

It is not easy to evaluate either the performance or the merit of a journalist, although the way dispatches are handled in a news agency is perhaps easier to measure quantitatively than other types of editorial work. None the less, the concept of performance is taken into account in certain systems for individual reports and corresponding bonus payments. The national collective agreement in Tunisia, for example, provides for a performance bonus based on a professional report which evaluates performance, professional know-how, application, punctuality and behaviour; this bonus cannot be granted if a serious misdemeanour has been committed or if the professional report fails to show a rating of at least ten out of 20 (article 46). In certain countries, these bonuses are paid in recognition of special work achievements rather than as a result of an overall evaluation: for example, in Ghana, an exclusive report; in Guyana, an outstanding article. In the Libyan Arab Jamahiriya, "production payments" are made for articles, studies and news reports made over and beyond the normal call of duty of the journalist, the amounts being fixed by the board of directors of the enterprise; if, during the course of their work, journalists publish important new documents, their remuneration is increased by 50 per cent. In addition to their fixed salary, journalists in the USSR are paid for their published work. Similarly, in Poland, any contribution made and accepted by the newspaper is taken into account and, if it exceeds the norm as mentioned above, it is paid on a special basis; these bonuses thus represent a form of author's royalties and a form of recognition for the productivity and ability of the journalist; they can also represent a substantial part of the total salary.

The "merit" bonus is for permanent work of a high standard rather than for an exceptional piece of work. It takes the form of a regular addition to the salary or a single payment at the end of the year. In Bulgaria, "highly creative journalists" receive what are known as "personal" salaries which amount to an addition of 20 per cent annually in relation to the normal scale; the honorary titles of "people's journalist" and "journalist emeritus" carry the right to a monthly bonus, as do scientific degrees if their holders are active in their specialised fields. In certain countries, bonuses are paid for linguistic qualifications, as for example in Bulgaria, Egypt, France, Poland and the USSR. A collective agreement in Canada stipulates that salaries above the minimum may be paid for individual merit and indicates that nothing need prevent employees from negotiating above established minimum salaries with the company.

Although not all agreements state that the employee is free to negotiate above the minimum salary scale, it is obvious that, whether described as a "merit bonus" or something else, additional individual payments are widespread in most countries. Theoretically they may be at the discretion of the employer, but in fact competition and the personal standing of the journalist are the determining factors. At times, the enterprise uses these extra payments as a means of getting round a governmental decision on income policy. Basic salaries are blocked or can only vary within authorised limits, but additional payments, which can be substantial and which are known only by the partners in these private and secret negotiations, reflect the real market rate of the journalist. In any event, the practice of additional individual payments has a disruptive effect on pay sheets, as may be imagined. However, to quote the words of the Advisory Conciliation and Arbitration Service in the United Kingdom, "many think them to be an inevitable part of the creative editorial environment, together with meteoric promotions and equally dramatic falls from grace".[9]

Allowances for professional expenses

In most countries, there are a whole range of allowances designed to reimburse journalists, in a lump sum or on the production of invoices, for the expenses they incur in the course of their activities. Essentially, they involve travel expenses, transport (including the use of their own cars), hotels and meals. It would be pointless to go into these matters in detail. Special allowances are usually paid for night work. Allowances for such personal items as camera equipment, typewriters and telephone are less common but are occasionally granted. Even less usual are allowances for clothing or a lump sum for petty expenses. In certain countries (India, Pakistan), housing allowances are paid. In Senegal, when journalists are assigned to places other than that in which they were recruited, and cannot find accommodation, their employer is responsible for housing them, but may deduct from their salary an amount equal to the average rate fixed by law. If journalists are sent abroad, they are entitled to a "foreign assignment allowance".

Another method used to cover professional expenses — but this time at the expense of the State and not the company — is tax reductions. In France, all journalists (as in a certain number of other professions) are allowed to deduct 30 per cent from their declared income and this amount is not subject to taxation. Other allowances for professional expenses — reporters' expenses, night taxis, end-of-year gifts — are also exempted from income tax. Any other items are regarded as covered by the 30 per cent tax reduction. Similar exemption systems are to be found in Austria, Denmark, the Federal Republic of Germany and Switzerland.

PAYMENT OF FREELANCE JOURNALISTS

As has been noted in Chapter 1, freelance journalists, or "stringers", are more vulnerable than others in terms of security and regular employment. Their position is no better as regards pay.[10] There are many countries where neither legislation nor collective agreements contain provisions for minimum fees. Freelance journalists are therefore obliged to negotiate payment for their contributions by themselves and it is therefore their reputation and the financial resources of the newspaper which determine the issue.

In other countries — Austria, France, the Netherlands, Switzerland, the United Kingdom, etc. — scales of payment are negotiated jointly or unilaterally by journalists' unions and members are expected to abide by them. But these are only minimum payments or guide-lines to serve as a basis for individual arrangements. In addition, most of these payment scales are based on the length of the story (according to the number of words) and its quality and fail to take into account the time spent on it or the difficulty of the work; in this respect, the collective agreement in French-speaking Switzerland is a notable exception. However, in some countries, extra payment is made for work at night and weekends. It goes without saying that stringers, by virtue of their independence from the newspapers and magazines they serve, do not receive any performance or merit bonuses and do not participate in profits in any of the other ways described above.

In short, with the exception of a few "star" stringers who are in a position to exploit their public image, freelance journalists are at a distinct financial disadvantage in comparison with journalists in regular employment.

WOMEN'S SALARIES

The above information concerns journalists of both sexes. While discrimination in salaries cannot be formally laid down in legislative measures or contractual arrangements, the reality is somewhat different. As in the career field, discrimination against women journalists takes insidious forms as far as pay is concerned. It can be seen as a logical result of the fact that women are generally employed in less well-paid jobs. It also arises from the fact that they are unfavourably treated by employers who are always free to exercise their right to pay journalists above the minimum rates. But since individual pay sheets are confidential, the exact degree of discrimination is not publicly known. However, a study published by UNESCO in 1979 leaves no doubt on the salary gap between men and women journalists.[11]

The study gives results of several investigations made during the seventies, particularly in North America and Europe. It shows — and probably the situation has hardly changed since that time — that, in the United States, women journalists, except those with important jobs on magazines, regularly received a lower salary than men for the same work. Among correspondents reporting on the work of the United States Congress, the average salary for women was only 58 per cent that of men. On the Canadian daily newspapers, women's salaries in each professional category were at the bottom of the scale. In Finland, Norway, Sweden and the United Kingdom, the investigations revealed a difference in pay, for equal qualifications, to the detriment of women. In France, according to a notice distributed in April 1982 by the Ministry for the Rights of Women — previously mentioned in Chapter 2 — the annual average salary paid to women journalists on one of the television channels was only 85 per cent that of their male colleagues. The same notice attributes this gap to the fact that women are less numerous in the highest-paid posts and does not mention journalists in the categories where wide disparities in pay are to be found for equal work.

* * *

The fact is that where the question of journalists' pay is concerned, leaving aside the special case of stringers, there is an infinite variety of situations. Pay seems to depend on a multitude of factors, both objective and subjective.

Among the objective factors, that is, those which can be measured or evaluated and thus enable salary scales to be fixed, those most commonly taken into consideration are the journalist's level of education, job, grade, specialisation, age and length of service; so far as the employers are concerned, the main factors considered are the type of newspaper or magazine, its circulation and turnover, its frequency of publication, its geographical location and the economic climate.

The subjective factors, that is, those which can be individually measured, are the personal qualities and reputation of the journalist and the strength of the union in collective bargaining on the one hand and, on the other, the margin of manoeuvre available to the employer and the willingness of the employer to use it.

It is the combination of these objective and subjective factors which determines the level of minimum salaries for each grade, the position occupied by each journalist in relation to these minimum rates and the additional pay a journalist may receive in the form of performance or merit bonuses.

The resulting obscurity of the situation rules out any reply to certain questions which naturally come to mind when studying the pay of a professional category, interesting as these questions may be: for example, what is the range of actual pay in journalism in a given country? Is this pay comparable to that of others in similar professions in the same country?

It would be even more pointless to try to compare journalists' pay in different countries in view of the numerous variables which would have to be taken into account.

Notes

[1] Royal Commission on the Press: *Final report*, op. cit., p. 42.

[2] "La Presse quotidienne", op. cit., p. 36.

[3] Labour Code, Article L.761-10.

[4] National Commission on Labour: *Report of the study group for the newspaper industry* (New Delhi, 1968), pp. 24-28; "Recommendations of the tribunals for working journalists and non-journalist newspaper employees, 12 August 1980", in *Indian Worker* (New Delhi), Mar. 1980.

[5] Vassilev, op. cit., pp. 65-77.

[6] Vassilev, loc. cit.

[7] Law No. 12908 of 1946, article 55.

[8] Vassilev, loc. cit.

[9] ACAS, op. cit., paragraph 587.

[10] See Lehni: *Economic and social conditions of freelance journalists*, op. cit.

[11] UNESCO: *News media: Image, role* ..., op. cit., pp. 56 ff.

SAFETY AND HEALTH 8

One of the journalists' unions which replied to the ILO investigation simply said, under the heading of "Safety and health": "Nothing special". Thus, in the eyes of this union, journalism offers no special risks to the safety or health of those who practise it. Perhaps the respondent had in mind only the normal circumstances of daily life and it has to be admitted that, in the statistics concerning occupational accidents and diseases, this profession does not loom large. However, it deserves a closer look.

SAFETY

In its annual report for 1977, the International Press Institute noted: "Journalism is fast becoming one of the world's riskiest professions." [1] To support this statement, it quoted assassinations carried out that year in six countries, bomb attacks in six countries, cases of torture and other forms of violence in eight countries, abductions in six and imprisonment in 21 countries. For the same year, Amnesty International listed 104 press correspondents who had disappeared or had been imprisoned in 25 countries.[2] The fact is that by virtue of their job journalists witness events which certain people feel they should be prevented from witnessing. To this end, they must be either intimidated or reduced to such a moral or physical state that they are unable to express their thoughts. Such practices are the result of certain political regimes and are a means of suppressing the freedom of the press when the truth could be dangerous for these regimes. They are also the acts of opponents of established authority when they feel that the exercise of this freedom is contrary to their plans and when they seek, as noted in the same report by the IPI, to draw attention to alleged political injustices.

Reporting on major catastrophes such as earthquakes involves an element of danger. Moreover, the mere fact that journalists are frequently moving about and using all kinds of transport involves a higher risk of accident (and illness) for reporters in the field than is the case with their colleagues in office jobs. But obviously, the most threatened journalists are war correspondents who do not hesitate to put their lives in danger to follow the action close-up, and who are thus just as exposed as the troops themselves. How many reporters, photographers and cameramen have paid heavily, not merely because of the need for information but also to satisfy the appetite of the reader or television viewer for dramatic accounts and pictures? Journalists assigned to "cover" mass demonstrations also sometimes run certain risks, although to a lesser degree, especially in exposing themselves and their equipment to rough treatment at the hands of over-zealous demonstrators and forces of order.

These different risks should certainly not be minimised. Indeed, they have been exposed by the interested parties themselves who are well placed to give them wide publicity. The fact remains that they affect only a minority of journalists — those who are placed in the exceptional circumstances described above. The conclusion reached by the IPI, which is probably exaggerated when such occupations as construction worker or coalminer are considered, should therefore be tempered by taking both sides into account; similarly, a more intermediate position should be taken by the union which finds nothing to report under the heading "Safety and health".

To find the happy medium, it is worth going back to the concept of "dangerous mission", a concept sufficiently limited to preserve its exceptional character, but wide enough to cover a variety of circumstances. A certain number of laws and collective agreements refer to this question, in explicit terms or otherwise, in order to lay down the principle of special protection. Such protection could consist, for example, of granting the right to journalists to refuse this type of mission if it resulted in the cancellation of their personal insurance policy; this is the case in Australia where journalists can even refuse to travel by air and where the employer is obliged to insure staff against accidents on air trips outside the regular commercial airlines, or in the course of work in militarily occupied zones. In Canada, a collective agreement authorises all journalists to refuse a mission if, on arrival at their destination, they find that it involves a danger of which they had no knowledge at the moment of their departure. The law in Argentina obliges the employer to take out a special insurance to cover exceptional risks of disease, invalidity or death. In Costa Rica, the College of Journalists has taken out a collective policy against professional risks. In Iraq, the law governing the practice of the profession stipulates that journalists should have life insurance cover, without prejudice to risk allowances and pensions in the event of invalidity or death. Under the terms of a collective agreement in Italy, foreign correspondents are entitled to receive a lump sum from their employer, each January, to cover the special risks in their

Safety and health

activity. The national collective agreement for working journalists in France provides for supplementary insurance for missions involving real danger *a priori*, and lists high risk circumstances: riot zones, civil wars, wars and military operations, regions affected by epidemics or natural disasters, reporting assignments underwater, in caves or in areas where there are high mountains, travel to unexplored regions and tests on engines or prototypes. In its model international contract, the International Federation of Journalists demands that journalists should have the right to refuse a dangerous mission, it being understood that their refusal in no case affects their career adversely.

Efforts have been made for several decades to provide members of the profession with certain immunities, both in their native country and abroad. An additional Protocol to the Geneva Conventions, signed on 12 August 1949, stipulated that journalists on dangerous professional missions in zones of armed conflict would be considered as civilians and protected as such, on condition that they engaged in no action calculated to affect their civilian status. The text provided for them to have a special identity card, but this project has not yet materialised for lack of agreement on an institution empowered to deliver such a document. The Final Act of the Conference on Security and Co-operation in Europe, held in Helsinki in 1975, contains a section on improving the conditions of work for journalists. More recently still, in 1978, the Twentieth Session of the General Conference of UNESCO adopted the Declaration on Fundamental Principles concerning the Contribution of the Mass Media to Strengthening Peace and International Understanding, to the Promotion of Human Rights and to Countering Racialism, Apartheid and Incitement to War. One of the clauses in this text (article II.4) states: "If the mass media are to be in a position to promote the principles of this Declaration in their activities, it is essential that journalists and other agents of the mass media, in their own country or abroad, be assured of protection guaranteeing them the best conditions for the exercise of their profession." Here again, the obstacles, in so far as principles and their application are concerned, are legion. Even the MacBride Commission considered it impossible to propose "special privileges to protect journalists in the performance of their duties, although journalism is often a dangerous profession. Far from constituting a special category, journalists are citizens of their respective countries, entitled to the same range of human rights as other citizens."[3]

At this level, journalists are reduced to trusting in their lucky star, or in the concept of human rights held by those they deal with and, when they are operating overseas, on the support of their embassies and the standing they enjoy if they manage to alert their embassy.

Profession: Journalist

HEALTH AND WELL-BEING

Some years ago, the International Organisation of Journalists carried out an inquiry among its member trade unions on the average longevity in the profession.[4] It revealed that in the USSR and Austria the average life expectancy of journalists was similar to that of the population at large, and, in Spain, to that of similar professions; that it was lower than in similar professions in Finland, the Federal Republic of Germany, Jordan and Sri Lanka and that it was below that of all other professions in Poland. However, the IOJ recognised the weakness of the results of its inquiry which, in the absence of official statistics on average longevity in the profession, apart from a special study on the subject in Poland, had been based solely on an estimate by the unions.

Such results would call for an explanation if they were scientifically confirmed: does a relatively high mortality rate correspond to a more or less high rate of accidents or morbidity, or both? And in this context, what is the degree of risk mentioned above in the section on safety? The answer to these questions would need long research for which there would seem to be no obvious justification. Perhaps it is more interesting to identify the illnesses which afflict journalists most frequently and to link them with the profession.

Those most often mentioned are cardio-vascular illnesses and, to a lesser extent, neuroses, followed by infections of the digestive tract and, in particular, liver complaints and gastric ulcers.

It is a natural temptation to connect these illnesses with the usual life-style of many journalists which is generally considered to be injurious to health. Irregular working hours, frequent night work, the interruption of weekly time off, undisciplined eating, anxiety or at least nervous tension due to the need to be abreast of the information and to work fast for fear of missing an important story or publishing one that has not been sufficiently checked, sharp competition, insecurity of employment, the frustrations inherent in the trade, the increased speed in computerised news agencies: these and other factors finally contribute to undermining the health of persons exposed to them and explain the relative frequency of heart attacks and nervous breakdowns in this profession.

Do journalists themselves regard their trade as a punishing one? There are divided opinions on this issue. An inquiry carried out in 1974 among a sampling of Austrian journalists [5] revealed that 37 per cent of them feared that their health would suffer from their conditions of work, but the remainder (63 per cent) had no anxiety on the matter. Judging from the results of an inquiry carried out in 1976 in Sweden by the Central Organisation of Salaried Employees among its members,[6] Swedish journalists would seem to be susceptible to mental strain: 48 per cent of them admitted they suffered from it often, 37 per cent occasion-

Safety and health

ally, 15 per cent rarely or never. They were thus behind teachers (60, 34 and 7 per cent, respectively), theatrical performers (50, 50 and zero per cent) and members of the police (49, 41 and 10 per cent). The corresponding figures for "white collar workers" were 32, 44 and 24 per cent.

The question was raised as to whether the new technology had any influence on the health of journalists. According to certain sources, they at least had a positive effect on physical working conditions, inasmuch as the installation of new equipment made it necessary to transform premises. For example, as was noted in a reply from Costa Rica, traditional news-rooms are often too small, badly lighted, very noisy and, in short, lacking in any comfort. When premises have to be rearranged so as to accommodate costly apparatus which requires optimal temperature and humidity, etc., it is obviously a good opportunity to apply modern standards of health, safety, ergonomics and comfort.

However, the use of certain types of equipment leads to a number of health problems. This is the case with video display terminals, in particular. Numerous complaints have been noted concerning eye-strain, changes in visual perception, watering of the eyes, dazzle, headaches and dizziness caused by prolonged reading on these screens; especially prominent are the difficulties experienced by those wearing spectacles, particularly bifocals; these were attributed to the heat and radiation emitted by the apparatus; after a long session in front of the screen, it was noted that performance declined, exemplified, for example, by a higher number of typographical errors. There have been many reports, as well as control studies and recommendations, published on this question. Here are some examples.

Two British specialists expressed the opinion that video display units are not injurious to vision, but they admitted that certain persons are not suited to work on this equipment. They recommended that eye tests should be carried out before assignment to the display terminal so as to detect any possible defects and that the operators should have regular examinations thereafter. They also recognised that by virtue of the fact that their vision is subjected to constant strain, the operators are more vulnerable than the average worker to different kinds of eye-strain such as fatigue, irritation, eye twitching, discomfort under strong light and headaches.[7]

In the United States, a report by the National Institute for Occupational Safety and Health established that operators of video display terminals showed a higher percentage of eye-strain, itching of the eyes and aching shoulders than average among other workers; but, according to this report, the radiation emitted by the apparatus was not high enough to be dangerous. The report recommends regular rest periods, initial and periodic eye tests, adjustable keyboards and screens, adjustment of room lighting to prevent glare and the testing of VDUs for radiation emissions before being used again after servicing. Thus, the

Profession: Journalist

Newspaper Guild issued instructions to its member unions to request breaks of 15 minutes after one hour of work on the console and 30 minutes after two hours.[8]

The joint Industrial Occupational Injury Institution in Hamburg and the Labour Ecology Research Centre at Geneva University have submitted detailed proposals for standards on working arrangements (the angle of keyboards and desks, the dimensions and positioning of working tables, the surface of the visual indicator, the height and spacing of lettering), the daily duration of work on the screen, the number and length of breaks, ophthalmological examinations and treatments, etc.[9]

It would seem relevant here to quote the recommendations made in this area by the ILO Advisory Committee on Salaried Employees and Professional Workers in January 1981, even though these are not directly intended for journalists:[10]

In designing work stations involving the utilisation of visual display units, particular attention should be paid to the following points:
- eye-strain: the eyesight of workers whose work involves the use of display screens should be checked before they are assigned to such work and if necessary periodically thereafter;
- fatigue: work should be so organised as to make the utilisation of screens over excessively long periods unnecessary. Workers may require adequate interruptions in work on visual display units;
- layout of work stations: this should be such as to avoid visual problems and postural pains. The screens should be regularly checked.

The proposed medical checks should not present serious difficulties in many countries where companies, legislation or collective agreements have made general medical examinations the rule; it would be enough to include eye tests in them. For example, the collective agreement for the press in Buenos Aires calls on companies to establish a system of periodical preventive medical examinations. The collective agreement in Finland stipulates that all journalists should have a complete medical check-up each year at the expense of their employer. In France, journalists, like all workers, are given check-ups when engaged and on return to work after illness; they are also subject to the general check-ups provided for in the Labour Code.

The presence of safety and health committees in press undertakings is calculated to encourage the safety and health protection of journalists and other staff. To cite just one example; in Japan, the Industrial Safety and Health Law of 1972 obliges companies to set up a committee responsible for safety and health, which includes one member of management, supervisors, a staff doctor and workers' representatives. It can be assumed that such bodies, when they function effectively, are as aware of the possible negative effects of the new technology as of other positive or negative elements in the working environment of news-rooms and composing shops.

Safety and health

But their influence is limited to the internal activity of the company, within the limits of the competence of such committees. Beyond that, journalists must be their own protectors: it is their responsibility, so far as circumstances allow, to discipline their life-style and, among other things, their eating habits.

Notes

[1] *IPI Report*, Monthly bulletin of the International Press Institute (Zurich), Jan. 1978, p. 3.

[2] The MacBride Commission: *Many voices, one world*, op. cit., p. 235.

[3] ibid., p. 264. The Commission was not, however, unanimous on this point and its chairman favoured a specific statute and protection (loc. cit., note 2).

[4] Vassilev, op. cit., pp. 121-127.

[5] *Massen-Medien in Österreich*, op. cit., p. 168.

[6] I. Wahlund and G. Nerell: *Work environment of white collar workers* (Stockholm, Central Organisation of Salaried Employees in Sweden, 1976), pp. 89-90.

[7] *Social and Labour Bulletin* (Geneva, ILO), No. 3/80, p. 340.

[8] ibid., pp. 340-341.

[9] *Social and Labour Bulletin*, No. 2/81, pp. 203-204 and pp. 206-208.

[10] ILO: *Note on the Proceedings*, Advisory Committee on Salaried Employees and Professional Workers, Eighth Session, Geneva, 1981; p. 31.

TERMINATION OF EMPLOYMENT 9

Termination of employment can come about on the initiative of the journalist (resignation) or of the employer (dismissal). These two aspects will be considered separately. A particular problem arising from the ethical standards in the profession — the conscience clause — has already been examined, together with the legal and contractual measures which relate to it.

The working relationship between journalist and employer can end in three types of circumstances: professional life comes to an end (retirement, invalidity, death), the journalist resigns or the journalist is dismissed. The first hypothesis is dealt with in the following chapter and is therefore not discussed here. Also left aside are cases of fixed-term contracts where the employment ends automatically on a fixed date, although this question is touched on in the general context of termination of work before the appointed time through resignation or dismissal.

RESIGNATION

In the section devoted to career mobility, the main reasons which could prompt journalists to leave a company or the profession of their own free will were listed.

General legislation, collective agreements or individual contracts usually oblige them to give their employer adequate notice. Table 9 shows that the period of notice in the event of resignation is rarely less than one month. It varies in certain countries, depending on the position occupied or the length of service, or both, and, in extreme cases, can reach eight months (Federal Republic of Germany). If they fail to respect this notice period, journalists lay themselves open to financial loss, either by having to sacrifice their salary for the period not covered by the notice, or by having to pay their employer a certain amount by way of compensation (Bulgaria, Sri Lanka, Switzerland).

Profession: Journalist

Table 9. Period of notice (resignation and dismissal)

Country	In case of resignation	In case of dismissal
Argentina		Up to 3 years of service: 1 month Beyond that: 2 months
Australia	Up to 26 weeks of service: 1 week Beyond that: from 2 to 16 weeks depending on grade and length of service	
Austria	1 month	3 months After 5 years of service, 1 month in addition for each year (maximum 12 months)
Belgium	3 months to 10 years of service 1 month in addition for each further year	6 months up to 10 years of service 1 month in addition for each further year
Brazil	1 month	1 month
Bulgaria	1 month	1 month
Canada		From 1 week to 3 months (depending on the company and the reason)
Czechoslovakia	3 months	3 months
Denmark	1 month	3 to 6 months
Ecuador	2 weeks	2 weeks
Egypt	1 month	
Finland	1 month	1 to 3 months depending on length of service
France	Up to 3 years of service: 1 month. Beyond that: 2 months	
Gambia	1 month	1 month
German Democratic Republic	2 weeks	2 weeks
Federal Republic of Germany	From 6 weeks to 8 months depending on length of service	
Hong Kong	1 month (more for senior positions)	1 month (more for senior positions)
India		6 months (editor-in-chief) 3 months (other journalists)
Ireland	1 week after 13 weeks of continuous service	From 1 week for less than 2 years of continuous service up to 8 weeks for 15 or more years of service
Italy	2 months	Compensation without prior notice
Japan		Compensation without prior notice
Jordan	1 month	1 month
Republic of Korea	1 month	1 month
Luxembourg	From 1 to 3 months according to length of service	From 2 to 6 months according to length of service

Table 9. (continued)

Country	In case of resignation	In case of dismissal
Madagascar	Up to 3 years of service: 1 month. Beyond that: 2 months	
Netherlands	3 months	3 months
New Zealand	8 weeks for a journalist of higher grade; 4 weeks for others	
Norway	8 weeks for a journalist of higher grade; 4 weeks for others	
Pakistan		From 1 to 3 months according to length of service
Poland	From 2 weeks to 3 months depending on length of service	
Senegal	Up to 3 years of service: 1 month. Beyond that: 2 months	
Sierra Leone	1 month for journalists paid monthly	1 month for journalists paid monthly
Sri Lanka	1 month notice (or forfeit of 1 month's salary)	Compensation without prior notice
Sweden	1 month 3 months after 8 years of service	3 months 8 months after 8 years of service
Switzerland	3 months	3 months
	(In French-speaking Switzerland, 2 months if the length of service is less than 2 years; 3 months, if it is from 2 to 10 years; 4 months if it is greater than 10 years)	
Tunisia	Up to 3 years of service: 1 month Beyond that: 2 months (according to the Labour Code) Period of notice equal to that of the length of the annual vacation (according to national collective agreement)	
Turkey	1 month	3 months (according to the law) 5 months (according to some collective agreements)
USSR	2 weeks	
United Kingdom	From 1 to 3 months depending on the position	From 1 to 3 months depending on the position
United States		2 or 4 weeks depending on the company and the reason

There are, however, circumstances which dispense with the need for notice: deciding to leave the job for health reasons (Poland, USSR); election to an official post or military call-up (USSR); or unilateral change in the contract of employment by the employer (Bulgaria).

Several documents provide for the payment of compensation to journalists on termination, even when they resign. In Argentina, for example, they are entitled to half a month's salary for each year of service above five years, with a maximum of three months, provided that they give the same period of notice as would be incumbent on the employer.[1] In Austria, compensation is from ten to 15 times the monthly salary, based on uninterrupted service.[2] In India, for at least ten years of continuous service, compensation is 15 days' pay for each year of service.[3] In Italy, there is length-of-service compensation equal to one month's salary for each year of service. For more than 15 years of service, the journalist also has the right to a lump-sum payment which varies from seven to 13 months' salary according to the post; the same applies to journalists who have reached the age of 55 with ten years of service and who resign to collect their pension.[4]

DISMISSAL

As with other workers, job security is a major preoccupation for journalists. Their security is now seriously threatened. The survival of the printed press was always precarious, but today it is constantly in danger through rising prices, competition from other communications media, mergers, takeovers and the rivalry of political and economic groups. Even newspapers which seemed invulnerable are now obliged to suspend publication, change ownership or disappear from the scene. What protection do journalists enjoy in such cases?

That this problem has become a matter of concern for legislators and parties to collective negotiations is only right and proper. In certain countries, job security is made a matter of principle. For example, the law in Argentina states: "The stability of the professional journalist, regardless of his title or position in the hierarchy, is the essential foundation of the present law." Under a Peruvian legislative decree of 1970, "journalists in the service of all press, radio and television enterprises, publicity agencies, national or foreign news agencies, press bureaux or other similar enterprises, enjoy stability of employment". But the real interest focused on the question is seen in the measures of protection which have been introduced, in the meticulous enumeration of the reasons justifying dismissal, in particular, and in the obligation on the employer to give dismissed journalists adequate notice and to compensate them in certain circumstances.

Grounds for dismissal

The grounds for justifiable dismissal which appear in the agreements are of three kinds.

The first relate to disciplinary procedures. They concern serious misdemeanour on the part of the employee, such as deliberate damage to the press undertaking, prolonged or repeated absences, serious or repeated displays of indiscipline, certain sentences pronounced by the courts and grave violations of the journalists' code of ethics.

Others deal with the physical or mental incapacity of the journalist to practise the profession and, in this context, certain agreements make mention of the risks of contagion. However, in this area, special measures are often taken to avoid abuse or arbitrary action. Thus, under the national collective agreement for press enterprises in Tunisia (article 39), when workers are judged to be physically unable to perform their work at the end of sick leave, they must undergo a medical examination by a staff doctor. If they disagree with the results, a second examination is carried out by two doctors, one chosen by management and the other by the worker; in the event of continued disagreement, the decision is taken by a third doctor chosen by the previous two. The termination of employment of workers stated to be unable to work becomes effective only if there are no other jobs available for them, despite their physical disability.

The third group of causes for valid dismissal are connected with the economic condition and organisation of the newspaper. In effect, this means reduction of staff due to measures of economy, reorganisation or mergers. It also applies to collective dismissals due to a stoppage of publication, or to the sale of the company, if the new owner does not retain the same editorial team. Also in this category is the elimination of posts or jobs caused by the adoption of new technology.

The latter point is of special concern to the journalists' unions who do not accept that the change-over to computers and photocomposition techniques justifies redundancies in the profession. In this respect, some of the collective agreements concluded in Canada are significant. One of them stipulates that no regular employees on the pay-roll on a certain date will lose their jobs during the agreed period on account of the introduction of new equipment or processes and that every effort will be made to lessen the impact of the new technology on the employees affected and to keep them at a level comparable to their previous ranking. The American agreements, while admitting that reduction in staff due to technological changes is a justifiable cause for dismissal, call on the employer to notify the union several months in advance and to effect these reductions by natural wastage. If redundancies are still unavoidable, they should be carried out in reverse order of seniority. Certain agreements sanction the privilege of "bumping", under which employees whose jobs are eliminated may claim posts in other categories if they are competent to occupy them and have more seniority than the former occupant, it being understood that the people who held those posts before may, in their turn, exercise the same privilege against yet other people. If any of the eliminated posts are re-established, the dismissed or transferred employees have first claim on them.

Chapter 3 contains other examples of agreements by which the parties engage to protect the interests of journalists apprehensive about the new printing and photocomposition techniques, even if they are not the category of workers most directly affected. The Declaration adopted by the International Federation of Journalists at its Congress in Nice in

1978 totally rejects redundancy on this level. It is interesting to observe that journalists' unions express themselves so forcefully on this point when, in their strategy on the subject of economic concentration, the accent seems to be mainly on the maintenance of plurality of sources of news; however, they do state that those who are unavoidably made redundant should be awarded the best possible terms.

There are other circumstances which, under the terms of texts in force, make the dismissal of journalists illegal. For example, in Chile, Law No. 17326 of 1970 forbids the dismissal of journalists during the 90 days before and the 120 days after a presidential election, without the authorisation of a labour tribunal. In Poland, the cancellation of a contract is impossible during the two years preceding the legal retirement age. In Hungary, this period is five years; moreover, in the same country, journalists with large families to support (at least four children), and without any source of revenue other than their salaries as journalists, cannot be dismissed; other circumstances which exclude dismissal are sickness leave, maternity leave, military service, etc. One television channel in the Federal Republic of Germany cannot dismiss employees after ten years of service unless their performance has deteriorated badly; even then, it must first offer them alternative posts corresponding to their abilities, or early retirement. In Bulgaria, journalists cannot be dismissed while carrying out union duties or for six months after they have given them up, except with the approval of the union.

Notice

As is shown in table 9, the period of notice in some countries in the event of dismissal is the same as for resignation. Three other countries included in this table (Italy, Japan, Sri Lanka) replace notice with compensatory severance pay. In Australia, Ireland, New Zealand and Senegal, notice can also be replaced by payment of the corresponding salary. In other countries, the notice period is longer when it is the employer and not the journalist who takes the initiative to terminate the employment. Two extreme cases should be noted: in Austria, the notice period can be as long as 12 months after 13 years of service, whereas the journalist who resigns need only give one month's notice; in Belgium, the notice period is six months up to ten years of service, with another month for each additional year. The period in the event of resignation is three months less.

The obligation to give notice does not apply when dismissal is effected for serious misdemeanour.

Conversely, the notice period is longer in certain countries if dismissal is part of a general staff reduction. In New Zealand, any journalist dismissed for economic reasons, closure of the publication, a merger, sale

Termination of employment

of the company or technological changes is given the normal notice of four to eight weeks depending on the post, plus the following periods: for at least six months of continuous service with the same newspaper, two weeks; for six months to one year, three weeks; for each additional year or part of a year, another week (or the corresponding salary if the employer or worker so desires). However, this clause is not applicable if a post with the same pay in the newly merged or restructured enterprise is offered to the journalist. A collective agreement in Canada obliges the employer to give one month's notice in cases of dismissal for economic reasons, whereas the notice for other reasons is two weeks; another agreement provides for three months' notice if dismissal is due to closure, sale or a merger. In the United States, the period of notice in one news agency is two weeks but is extended to four weeks in the event of staff reductions.

The clauses regulating the notice period sometimes include a measure which authorises dismissed journalists to spend part of their normal working time looking for a new job before the expiration of their contract. Such measures are in effect in Argentina, France, the Federal Republic of Germany, Senegal and Tunisia, among other countries.

Severance pay

The measures concerning the obligation of the employer to compensate the dismissed journalists are as varied as those which regulate the period of notice in different countries. Certain countries do not treat this professional category any more favourably than other employees. Many others, as shown in table 10, give the journalist a better deal. For example, an Italian journalist with a long period of service collects payment for a considerable number of months. Admittedly, the journalist receives no notice. But in most other countries the obligation to award severance pay for dismissal goes with that of giving notice or is replaced by a corresponding payment. This can be cancelled in certain circumstances: for example, a grave misdemeanour by the journalist, or the offer of a satisfactory new job (Australia, Federal Republic of Germany). Table 10 sets out only the general measures without entering into detail on their conditions of application which can sometimes be complex. It is obvious that individual contracts can stipulate higher severance pay than is awarded by the terms of agreements, particularly for senior journalists.

The model contract which the International Federation of Journalists has proposed for its affiliated organisations to follow in their negotiations states that a journalist should be given at least three months' notice on dismissal by the employer. The same contract stipulates that, if dismissal is not due to a serious misdemeanour by the person con-

Profession: Journalist

Table 10. Severance pay in case of dismissal or redundancy

Argentina	1 month's salary per year of service
Australia	4 weeks' salary (if the journal ceases publication)
Austria	From 2 to 15 months' salary depending on the length of service
Canada	1 week of salary for 5 or 6 months of continuous service depending on the company (with a maximum of 42 to 52 weeks); lump sum in addition according to one collective agreement
Ecuador	From 2 to 12 months' salary, plus 25 per cent of monthly salary per year of service
Finland	Lump sum payment for a journalist over 50 years of age laid off for economic reasons
France	1 month's salary per year of service up to 15 years. Beyond that, lump sum fixed by arbitration tribunal
Federal Republic of Germany	From $1^1/_2$ to 6 months' salary depending on the length of service and age
Greece	1 to 18 months' salary depending on length of service
India	15 days' salary per year of service
Italy	Management: 13 months' salary Editor-in-chief: 10 months' salary Section head: 8 months' salary Other journalists: 7 months' salary Plus 1 month per year of service, plus 1 month if service has been more than 20 years
Japan	Lump sum varying with the length of service according to a formula fixed by each company
Jordan	1 month's salary per year of service
Madagascar	1 month's salary per year of service up to 15 years. Beyond that a decision is made by the Tribunal
Philippines	1 month's salary per year for the first 20 years of service, and $^1/_2$ month for each of the following years (according to a collective agreement)
Senegal	30 per cent of monthly salary for each of the first 5 years of service 35 per cent of monthly salary for each of the 5 following years 40 per cent of monthly salary beyond the 10th year
Spain	1 month's salary per year of service
Tunisia	According to the law, 1 month's salary per year of service up to 15 years. Beyond that, an arbitration tribunal will decide According to the national collective agreement, the calculation of the severance pay is made on the basis of the annual vacation length; it cannot be less than the average monthly salary during the previous 12 months, nor greater than 15 monthly salaries
United Kingdom	1 month's salary per year of service
United States	In a news agency: from 2 weeks' salary for 6 months of service to 75 weeks for 396 months or more In other fields: from 2 weeks' salary for the first 6 months of service to 72 weeks for 426 months or more

cerned, the employee should receive severance pay on the basis of one month's salary for each year of service with the same newspaper, and a much higher rate after 15 years of service. It also stipulates that the same compensation should be guaranteed if journalists resign because of a change in the political line of the newspaper which offends their conscience.

As can be seen, the measures in effect in a large number of countries are not far from those which the International Federation of Journalists considers as the norm, both for notice and for severance pay. Some even go further.

The substantial advantages that go with seniority seem to have found general acceptance in many countries. This is especially true in cases where employment is terminated on account of "a change of policy". It might be asked whether severance pay awarded in application of the "conscience clause" — theoretically a powerful instrument of protection — is so complicated to determine that it runs the risk of becoming inoperative in practice. Faced with the prospect of having to pay considerable compensation, the enterprise could be tempted to use every device to frustrate the application of this clause.

But the main weakness of these measures is that they cover only permanent staff and leave freelance journalists without any protection. More often than not, they are simply ignored and sometimes specifically excluded from the application of these measures. In Austria, Belgium, Finland, Luxembourg, the Netherlands, Turkey, the United Kingdom and the United States, they have no protection against dismissal.[5] They are not entitled to any notice or severance pay except in a very few countries and, even then, their collaboration must be regular enough to place them on the same level as part-time or temporary workers (Denmark, France, Norway, Sweden, Switzerland). In most cases, they have no protection unless they have managed to negotiate an individual contract. It would therefore appear that special efforts should be made on their behalf, even if, as with independent workers in general, the very nature of their employment makes the improvement of their situation difficult.

Notes

[1] Law No. 12908 of 1946, article 46.

[2] *Massen-Medien in Österreich*, op. cit., pp. 171-172.

[3] Law of 1955: Working Journalists (Conditions of Service) and Miscellaneous Provisions Act, article 5.

[4] National agreement of 1977, Article 27.

[5] Lehni: *Economic and social conditions of freelance journalists*, op. cit., pp. 32-33.

SOCIAL SECURITY   10

Journalists need protection against illness just as other workers do. Some of them are exposed to risks during their working lives. Their profession is not immune to unemployment. And all journalists dream of having sufficient resources to enjoy a decent existence when they are too old to practise their profession.

The study on journalists carried out by the ILO 50 years ago revealed that they were virtually without protection in this area. It states that the journalist is "more often than not, left to his own resources. He is generally excluded from the scope of the laws on compulsory insurance, either because he is a professional worker or because his salary exceeds a certain maximum figure fixed by law".[1]

Since that time, retirement pension schemes have flourished and, in most cases, journalists have been included in one or other of the numerous schemes which protect the vast majority of workers.

In many countries, journalists, or at least some of them, enjoy the benefits of an overall system for all eventualities, usually for illness, accidents or retirement. This applies to all the socialist countries and also to Argentina, Austria, Belgium, Brazil, Costa Rica, Denmark, Ecuador, Egypt, Finland, France, the Federal Republic of Germany, Ghana, Guyana, Honduras, Ireland, Japan, Malaysia, New Zealand, Pakistan, the Philippines, Senegal, Spain, Sri Lanka, Sweden, Tunisia and the United Kingdom. This list is not exhaustive but it is an indication of the progress made over the last 50 years.

This is obviously not the place to detail the various schemes. In any case, their formulas vary to such an extent that it would be difficult to summarise them. The following remarks therefore merely cover certain aspects of schemes peculiar to the profession which, for the most part, are complementary to a general scheme which in itself is inadequate, although some of these constitute the sole or the main protection for journalists, in the absence of an overall scheme. They have been established by legislation, collective agreement or arbitration findings.

Profession: Journalist

In the Federal Republic of Germany, salaried journalists whose pay is below a certain level are compulsorily linked to the legally established medical insurance scheme; if their salary exceeds this level, they can opt to remain in this scheme. Accident insurance, also compulsory, covers the risks of invalidity and death in the event of occupational accidents or professional illness. For reporters on dailies and periodicals, old-age insurance is supplemented by the profession's own system which has been established by collective agreement.

In Australia, if a journalist's salary reaches a level at which the law on accidents at work is no longer applicable, it is incumbent on the employer, regardless of the amount, to pay the medical costs and allowances provided for in this law. Most of the large companies have their own retirement schemes. In the State of Victoria, sick leave is paid in the following manner: up to six months' employment, one week at full salary, from six months to five years, four weeks at full salary, then four weeks at 50 per cent of salary, and four weeks at 25 per cent of salary; after five years, six weeks of full salary, then four at 50 per cent, and finally four at 25 per cent (certain newspapers offer more favourable conditions).

In Austria, collective agreements guarantee journalists, in the event of illness, payment of their full salary for a period of from one-and-a-half to six months, depending on their length of service, then 49 per cent for a period of from one to four months unless they qualify for an invalidity or retirement pension.

In the United Republic of Cameroon, civil service journalists enjoy free consultations and out-patient care in hospitals; all medical care for illnesses attributable to work is also free.

In Canada, companies generally subscribe to provident schemes and life insurance policies for which they pay the total contributions due on behalf of their staff. In the event of sick leave, journalists continue to receive their salary for a period and at a level which varies according to the company: for example, one formula provides for full salary for six months and 50 per cent thereafter; another for full salary for the first week of the first and second period of sick leave in the year, and two-thirds of the full salary for the first week of the third sick leave period. There are also pension funds to which the employer and employee contribute equally, for example, each paying 5 per cent of the monthly salary.

In Chile, the national pension fund for civil servants and journalists provides medical care for its members and subsidises 50 per cent of the medical expenses of companies which have their own medical service. It also pays retirement benefits as well as life insurance payments in two forms: a single payment of a capital sum equal to two years of salary or pension, and payment of a monthly amount equal to at least 50 per cent of the salary or pension for one month and increasing with the number of years over which contributions have been made.

Social security

In Finland, journalists on sick leave receive the whole of their salary for three months, and then 50 per cent in the following three months. They are entitled to one medical examination a year at the expense of their employer, and a life insurance policy, also at the employer's expense.[2]

In France, journalists who have worked for a period of six months to one year in the company have the right to full salary for two months and two months at half salary when absent through sickness or an accident at work; three months at full salary and three months at half salary after one year of service; four months at full salary and four months at half salary after five years of service; five months at full salary and five months at half salary after ten years of service; and six months at full salary and six months at half salary beyond 15 years of service. There are also a certain number of retirement schemes which complement the general scheme, in particular a retirement fund for press executives for which contributions are based on that part of the salary between the ceiling for social security and another ceiling four times higher, and another fund for senior executives, without any ceiling. Senior executives can thus collect a total pension equal to 80 per cent of their last salary. Journalists also benefit from a complementary unemployment fund. Until 1981, contributions to this fund — and consequently the amounts insured — were based on the salary less the tax allowance (30 per cent) mentioned earlier in connection with allowances for professional expenses; since 1981, the total salary has been taken into account.

In Iraq, press undertakings enter into a complete insurance contract for their journalists for the whole period of their employment. A pension is paid to any journalist with 15 years of service who is 50 years of age, or to any journalist with 25 years of service regardless of age.

Since 1926, social security for journalists in Italy has been entrusted to a single organisation designed for them: the Giovanni Amendola National Pension Fund Institute. Its statutes, which have been amended several times, give it extensive powers: besides managing funds for the main risks (invalidity, old age, death, sickness, occupational accidents, unemployment, maternity), it provides other forms of aid such as educational scholarships for the children of journalists, or assistance in housebuilding. It is sufficient to mention here two examples of the amounts insured by this Institute. The first concerns old-age pensions of which the annual amount is equal to one-thirtieth of 80 per cent of the annual salary, subject to contributions for each year of contribution calculated on the most favourable of the following bases: the last 60 months of contribution or the ten highest-paid calendar years. The second example concerns compensation for involuntary unemployment: this compensation is paid for a maximum of 450 days, including legal holidays, and is equal for each day to one-thirtieth of 60 per cent of the average monthly salary, subject to contribution payments calculated for the last three months.

Profession: Journalist

In Japan, where journalists, like other workers, are obliged to be affiliated to insurance schemes for health insurance, unemployment, old-age and occupational accidents, some of the major press and television groups have set up private pension funds. Their purpose is either to complement the amounts paid through the general scheme or to fill the gap between the compulsory retirement age (which varies according to the company) and the age of entitlement under the general scheme (60 years for men and 55 for women). For example, a magazine which has set the retirement age at 60 pays a pension to journalists who retire at 55 or more, after 15 years or more of service. A television network where the normal retirement age is 55 grants a pension to journalists who retire at 55 or later, after 15 years or more of service, until they reach the age of 60. In both cases, the system is financed solely by the company.

The general scheme in New Zealand ensures compensation in case of accident, covers the medical costs caused by the accident, and pays old-age pensions from the age of 60. Some newspapers have their own retirement schemes which provide for the payment of a lump sum — equivalent to three or four years' salary — on the date of retirement; but the rights acquired within the framework of these schemes are not transferable in the event of a change of employer. Moreover, some newspapers take out life insurance or health insurance policies, or both, for their staff. Each year of service with the same employer earns the right to ten days of paid sick leave, cumulative up to a total of 150 days.

In Pakistan, the law makes it obligatory for all newspapers employing at least 20 persons to take out a group insurance policy to cover risks not included in the general scheme, specifically death from natural causes and invalidity. The premiums are carried by the employer. The National Press Trust Organisation has established an old-age insurance scheme which makes payments to journalists of 60 years of age and over.

In the United Kingdom, there is a variety of pension schemes. The general basic pension paid by the State is supplemented by a pension linked to salary, to which amounts paid by a company insurance scheme, contributory or otherwise, can be added. This scheme may or may not be combined with the state pension scheme. The result is that total payments on retirement can range from 25 to 90 per cent of salary, depending on the scheme applied. The National Union of Journalists estimates that two-thirds of its members are covered by company insurance schemes.

The national collective agreement in Senegal provides that, until a compulsory health, surgical and maternity insurance scheme is established, companies must take out insurance to cover these risks, with reimbursement of at least 80 per cent of the expenses involved. Salaried staff pay only half the contributions. Paid sick leave varies from one month at full salary for one year's service to six months at full salary and six months at half salary for 20 years of service. Retirement payments made

Social security

under the general scheme are supplemented by those paid by the scheme for executives. In the event of death, the beneficiaries receive compensation equal to one-half of the amount the journalist would have been entitled to in the case of dismissal.

In Sierra Leone, where all workers are insured under a general scheme, journalists collect their full salary for the first six weeks of sick leave and half salary for the following six weeks. Maternity leave is three months (six weeks before and six weeks after the birth), at half salary.[3]

In the French-speaking part of Switzerland, the payment in the event of absence from work through sickness amounts to 100 per cent of the salary for the first 121 days and 80 per cent from the 122nd to the 365th day. Once journalists have used up their right to the sickness payment, they must work for at least two years to recover the benefit. The publisher insures them against accidents, at work or elsewhere; in the first case, it is the company which pays the premium. After one year of work, maternity leave is 14 weeks on full salary plus 12 weeks without pay. The publisher pays one-half of the reporter's insurance premium for medical care and pharmaceutical costs, subject to a fixed maximum. The publisher also contributes 6 per cent of the journalist's minimum salary to legally established schemes for retirement, invalidity and death.

In Tunisia, the Secretary of State for Information and Planning prepares an annual list of enterprises which assume the obligation to pay their staff, in the event of illness, full salary for a month and half salary for the two following months if length of service is between six months and one year, and full salary for at least three months and half salary for the following three months if length of service exceeds one year.[4] The national collective agreement for the press stipulates that a group insurance be taken out by the employers and interested workers as a supplement to the national social security fund.

In the socialist countries, journalists enjoy the benefit of free medical aid as do all other workers.[5] However, in several of these countries, they have to contribute to the cost of medicaments obtained outside hospitals (15 per cent in Bulgaria, 30 per cent in Poland, for example). They have access to dispensaries or polyclinics attached to publishing groups (Bulgaria, USSR), to the Union of Journalists (Czechoslovakia), or to enterprises and unions jointly (Poland). In Hungary, within the general framework of the combined unions' social insurance services, journalists have their own special insurance section, equipped with its own medical services. In Poland, they enjoy a better retirement scheme than average: they have the right, without obligation, to retire at 60 years of age for men and 55 for women, five years earlier than other workers; moreover, after 15 years of service, they receive an increased pension (1.5 per cent more annually). Also to be noted are the rest homes for journalists (in Bulgaria, Czechoslovakia, Hungary and the USSR, for example), not to mention the homes or care centres run by the International Organisation of Journalists in Bulgaria, Czechoslovakia and Hungary, which welcome journalists from all over the world.

This brief look at some of the aspects of social security for journalists still leaves the particular situation of freelance journalists unresolved. As has been seen, they are at a disadvantage on several levels in comparison with staff journalists and they are no better off where social security is concerned.[6] Regulations on their situation vary considerably from one country to another, ranging from the lack of any genuine protection to a situation akin to that of salaried staff. In this context, it is interesting to note the measures taken in three European countries to improve the lot of the freelance journalist.

In the Federal Republic of Germany, a law on the social security of artists, adopted on 27 July 1981 and effective as of 1 January 1983, includes journalists and writers if they are not covered under any other scheme. Contributions are based on the net income of the persons insured. They contribute half of the premium, calculated on the basis of 5 per cent of their income. A third is contributed by a federal subsidy and the other two-thirds by the business partners of the artists and authors: publishers, news agencies, theatres, art galleries, radio networks, etc. The coverage is for illness and old age.

In France, a law of 9 August 1963 obliges professional journalists and related workers — whose articles, news reports, illustrations and pictures are paid for on a lineage or space basis — to be affiliated to the social insurance services, regardless of their legal links with the press company (article 242 of the Social Security Code). By agreement, their contributions are calculated at a rate one-third lower than that applied to salaried staff. Since 1963, freelance journalists have been able to join complementary retirement fund schemes through a system of "retirement points" which takes into account their individual working relationships.

In the French-speaking part of Switzerland, the publisher is obliged to pay the contributions legally due from an employer, regardless of the method of paying, or the status of, a freelance journalist who is on the professional register. The publisher participates in the financing of the complementary retirement scheme of the Swiss Federation of Journalists by contributing an amount corresponding to 4 per cent of the total fees paid to the freelance journalist in the preceding year. The latter pays the same amount, subject to a fixed minimum.

* * *

It should again be said that the picture given above does not claim to be complete. In fact, the expression "social security" covers a whole mosaic of schemes in most countries and in numerous professions, and journalism is a good illustration of this variety. But the essential point is to assess whether that social security cover is satisfactory.

Social security

It is obviously impossible to give an exact opinion on the matter, since any evaluation has to take into consideration the national circumstances and the situation in other professions. The general impression that emerges is that there is marked inequality between different countries, between newspapers and also between various categories of journalists, particularly with regard to certain risks. There is no common denominator, for example, between the case of an editor of a major newspaper in a given country who, through a combination of the general scheme and several complementary schemes, retires with a pension equal to 80 per cent of a substantial salary, and the case of a simple reporter who, in another country, leaves with a meagre pension because there is no complementary scheme or because he or she has worked for several different companies successively and the rights acquired with each have not been transferable.

It is therefore not surprising that the model contracts proposed by certain union organisations to their members lay great emphasis on this question. This explains why the International Federation of Journalists recommends in the case of sickness that journalists should continue to receive their salary for at least six months, that at the age of 65 at the latest they should be entitled to a pension equivalent to at least two-thirds of their salary and that this pension should be linked to salary increases. It is clear that, despite the progress made in the last 50 years, social security cover for journalists against illness and old age, not to mention other risks, has not reached the desired level and that, in certain countries at any rate, there is a long way to go.

Notes

[1] ILO: *Conditions of work and life of journalists*, op. cit., p. 174.

[2] *IFJ Information* (Brussels, International Federation of Journalists), Vol. XXXI, 1981, p. 2.

[3] Oyelude, op. cit., p. 139.

[4] Law No. 66-27 of 30 April 1966, article 406.

[5] Vassilev, op. cit., pp. 138 ff.

[6] See, among others, Lehni: *Economic and social conditions of freelance journalists*, op. cit., pp. 32-36; and the International Federation of Journalists: *Report of the working group on freelance journalists* (Brussels, Nov. 1977; mimeographed).

INDUSTRIAL RELATIONS 11

No matter how inclined they may be to individualism by virtue of their work and the habits of their profession, journalists are still in most cases members of a team — the editorial team — and, furthermore, they are members of the overall staff of a newspaper. They thus have interests in common with other salaried staff and in most cases these interests can be better protected through collective action. Moreover, a newspaper is an enterprise and, as in other enterprises, the relations between social partners are organised according to patterns which evolve gradually and are then fixed through laws and regulations conceived for the profession but often having a general significance.

Thus, the foregoing description of the employment problems and working conditions of journalists can be usefully rounded off with a general look at the relations between newspaper managements and editorial staff. To this end, an attempt will be made to show some aspects of collective agreements in the press and of the mechanisms designed to settle labour disputes and, finally, to present in broad outline some of the ways in which journalists participate, directly or indirectly, in the decision-making process in their enterprise.

TRADE UNIONISM AMONG JOURNALISTS

Lenin was a member of the Union of Journalists in the USSR and was the holder of card no. 1. Not all journalists' unions can pride themselves on such illustrious figures, even though it may be found in the future that well-known people began by being militant in the ranks of one or another of these unions. But this does not in any way detract from, or add to, the vitality of unionism within this profession in a large number of countries.

As with other categories of professional workers, for many years journalists felt that their professional interests were too far removed from the interests of manual workers to be protected by the same methods. This explains the appearance in Europe in the second half of the nineteenth century and at the beginning of the twentieth century of a number of associations with various objectives: the establishment of friendly links, the exchange of professional information, mutual aid and social provident funds, the creation and observation of ethical standards, etc. But gradually the need was felt for appropriate instruments to conduct collective bargaining on conditions of work: hence the progressive transformation of these associations into real trade unions, or the creation of new types of trade union organisation.[1]

For example, the Swiss Press Association, originally founded in 1883 as a simple corporate grouping, concluded collective agreements with the Publishers' Association when it was founded in 1900. The Swedish Federation of Journalists, created in 1901, devoted itself to the protection of the financial interests of its members, while the older organisation, the Press Association (1874), continued to confine itself to maintaining friendly relations. Equally, the Association of Journalists in Copenhagen, founded in 1900, concentrated on the protection of the professional interests of its members, whereas an older organisation, the Association of Journalists, was mainly concerned with ensuring that its members obtained retirement pensions. In the United Kingdom, the National Union of Journalists, founded in 1907, quickly adopted the methods of a trade union, thus taking on a different character from that of the Institute of Journalists which had been established in 1890 and which only became a trade union much later. The National Association of the German Press, founded in 1910, also later became an active trade union; in 1922, together with the Employers' Association for the Newspaper Industry, it created a joint national commission for collaboration, as a result of which the two organisations achieved a great deal of progress in terms of working conditions and state insurance. The Italian National Press Association, created in 1910, quickly succeeded in negotiating a collective contract for the profession. The Vienna Press Organisation, from its foundation in 1917, assumed the protection of the material interests of its members and negotiated collective agreements. Other non-trade union organisations, including one that had been in existence since 1860, disappeared. The Union of French Journalists, founded in 1918, functioned as an instrument of social progress from the start, just as its name would imply, although its efforts in the field of working conditions did not achieve all that was expected.

Some of these organisations still exist, despite various ups and downs and changes of name (for example, the Swiss Press Association became the Swiss Federation of Journalists in 1976). Many others have emerged in all continents and have today spread to virtually all countries. It should be noted, however, that in certain developing countries, such organisations have no real negotiating powers. This is somewhat surprising since journalists' associations in developing countries could have developed rapidly and bypassed the laborious evolution of their predecessors in the industrialised countries. But the fact that they have not is perhaps understandable in certain countries in the light of such factors as restrictive legislation, the small numbers of journalists and the indifference of many professional workers to the idea of trade unions in general.

At a time when trade union freedom is under serious and repeated threats, it is obvious that journalists cannot remain immune to this kind of violation of basic rights. The monthly bulletin of the International Federation of Journalists makes regular mention of the detention of journalists involved in trade union activity, but it is not easy to say whether they have been arrested as journalists or as trade unionists. There is little doubt that, by virtue of their role as informants, journalists represent a favourite target for certain political regimes, as mentioned in Chapter 8, and any activity as trade unionists only serves to expose them further. It is doubtful if the Committee on Freedom of Association of the International Labour Office — the body responsible for examining complaints on the violation of trade union rights — has been confronted with any cases relating to a specific journalists' union, but a certain number of allegations have been brought to its attention on the arrest, death in detention, torture, persecution and expulsion of journalists.

In any case, for journalists, as for all other professional groups, the full exercise of trade union rights remains an objective which is never easy to achieve and which is often put to the test by changing circumstances at national or company level. There are numerous ways in which these rights can be violated without recourse to such brutal actions as those mentioned above. The International Federation of Journalists did not consider it unnecessary to insert a clause in its international model agreement stipulating that an employer must not prevent a journalist from joining a trade union or accepting a trade union assignment. Certain collective agreements are more precise on the question. Under the terms of the national collective agreement in Senegal (article 7), the contracting parties recognise that journalists and their employers have the freedom to associate for the collective defence of their interests as journalists or employers, and trade unions have the same rights to pursue their activities within the context of the legislation in force. Employers bind themselves not to be influenced by the fact that employees are, or are not, members of a professional association or trade union when they make decisions on their conduct or workload, disciplinary measures, promotion and dismissal. For their part, employees bind themselves not to bring any pressure or constraints to bear on their colleagues to force them to join any trade union organisation. The same agreement guarantees union delegates facilities for carrying out their work, time to carry it out, notice boards, etc. The Tunisian agreement is similar on these points, but also describes the guarantees enjoyed by the union delegate where promotion and social benefits are concerned.

Other texts go even further and make membership of a specific union a condition for recruitment and continued employment; this is what is known as the "closed shop", meaning an enterprise which only takes on employees who belong to a given union. Such a situation applies to companies in Canada, New Zealand and the United States where the collective agreement contains a clause providing for the automatic deduction of union fees from the salary.

In the United Kingdom, the subject of trade union monopoly has given rise to sharp controversy. For some, such a practice among journalists is an attack on the freedom of expression. For others — in particular the National Union of Journalists — nothing is more important than strengthening the power of the union for negotiating salaries and working conditions. The law of 1976 which modified legislation on trade unions and labour relations [2] is neutral on this matter: it does not prohibit the closed shop, but nor does it make it obligatory. It is up to the social partners to reach an understanding on the adoption or rejection of this practice and on the conditions and exceptions to be applied. However, the legislators were not unaware of the risk inherent in a trade union monopoly of the freedom of expression, since article 2 of the law of 1976 requested the parties to establish jointly, within 12 months, a charter of practical guidance on questions relating to the freedom of the press, failing which the Government would submit its own charter project to Parliament. As the employers and journalists were unable to reach agreement on a text, the Royal Commission on the Press, in its report of 1977, deemed it essential to recommend a certain number of safeguards to the Government, notably:

(a) Freedom of a journalist to act, write and speak in accordance with conscience without being inhibited by the threat of expulsion or other disciplinary action by his union or his employer.

(b) Freedom for an editor of a newspaper, news agency or periodical to accept or reject any contribution whether or not the contributor is a professional journalist or a member of a union, so long as this freedom is not abused.

(c) Freedom for an editor to join or not to join any union and, if a member of a union, to take part or not to take part in any industrial action called for by the union.[3]

In practice, many company agreements in the United Kingdom contain a clause which more or less encourages membership of a union. Others are limited to the recognition of the right of journalists to join the union of their choice or, subject to the law, to remain outside any union. Certain newspaper managers oppose any proposal calculated to establish a union monopoly in their company.[4]

In these circumstances, it is hardly surprising that the level of trade unionism is extremely high — nearly 100 per cent. Similar figures are to

Industrial relations

be found in other countries where membership of a trade union is in practice obligatory (New Zealand, United States) or encouraged by the social structure (Sweden). But in fact, in most countries, it is difficult to discover the level of trade unionism among journalists, either because the unions are reluctant to reveal the number of their members, or because the figures are buried in more general statistics. By way of illustration, here are some estimates: Brazil, 90 per cent; the Netherlands, 85 per cent; Austria, 70 to 80 per cent; Barbados, 70 per cent; France, 40 to 60 per cent.

In other countries, the situation varies considerably from one establishment to another. Moreover, when journalists do not have their own organisation, any estimate becomes approximate at establishment level and impossible at national level. Japan is a typical case in this respect. There the employees are organised within each company, and the rate of trade unionism ranges from 10 to 90 per cent. Since journalists join the same company trade union as other employees, it is obviously hard to count them at the national level.

The existence of a single or largely predominant trade union for journalists is characteristic of many countries: for example, Australia, the United Republic of Cameroon for the private sector (journalists in the public sector are not organised, although trade union freedom for public servants is recognised), Canada, Ireland, Italy, Kuwait, the Netherlands, Sweden, the United States and the socialist countries. In France, where trade union pluralism is as evident in this branch as in others, the four most important unions have grouped themselves into a National Union of Journalists, a body for co-ordination and action; this body has a *de facto* structure but no legal entity, since the central organisations for workers do not allow their members to belong to another union.

It should also be noted that radio and television journalists are sometimes organised separately: they either set up their own union, as in Finland or the Federal Republic of Germany, or join existing unions in other branches, for example, the Public Service Association in New Zealand. In Sweden, they may be members of both the Swedish Journalists' Union and the Swedish Union for Industrial Employees.

One final point worthy of attention concerns the relations between journalists' unions and other trade unions, particularly those in comparable branches. There are often structural links between them, in the sense that journalists' unions and typographers' unions, for example, are both affiliated to one major national confederation. But this is not always the case: in Sweden, for example, typographers belong to the main workers' organisation — the Swedish Central Organisation of Workers — whereas journalists are affiliated to the Swedish Confederation of Trade Unions which also groups together bank and commercial employees. The Danish Union of Journalists is absolutely autonomous, as is the Swiss Federation of Journalists. Thus, relations are established directly between the unions involved, both at national level and at company level.

In Chapter 3, it was noted how the adoption of new composing and printing techniques had, in many countries, induced journalists' unions and typographers' unions to seek joint agreement on this issue, although their interests are partly in conflict and partly in common. But there are also permanent procedures for co-operation. The Association of Hungarian Journalists concluded a co-operation agreement in 1970 with the Printing, Paper and Press Workers' Union and with the Federation of Art Workers' Union: the three organisations act jointly, for example, in the defence of the interests of their members, in the preparation of legislative texts on mass communications, or in studying plans for the development of radio and television information services; meetings are held every six months between their managements.[5] In most British newspapers, the different trade union sections of the various undertakings, the "chapels", amalgamate into federated bodies, each endowed with their own funds and written rules, but with authority usually limited to questions of general well-being, each section preserving its full independence where negotiations on conditions of work are concerned.

It is particularly difficult for journalists' unions and printers' unions to reach an understanding when their vital interests are at stake, whether it concerns the interests of each of these professional categories or those of newspaper owners. This was evident at the time of the major conflicts which shook Fleet Street for several years or those which paralysed the press in the United States in 1978. But in the latter country, the journalists went on strike in support of the typographers whose employment was threatened by automation. This was due to the negotiations in 1975 between the union of the journalists and that of the typographers with a view to a merger of the two organisations; however, the length of the negotiations shows how difficult it is to surmount obstacles caused by different structures and traditions.

International organisations

This section would be incomplete without a few further words on the two great organisations which, on the international level, take under their umbrella most of the national unions for journalists.

The International Federation of Journalists is the younger of the two if its formal date of birth, 1952, is taken as the yardstick. But in fact it had a predecessor of the same name, created in 1926 and dissolved in 1940. Under its new form, the Federation, which has no political or ideological aims, pursues the following objectives:
— to protect the freedom of the press and that of journalists and to uphold the standards of the profession;

Industrial relations

- to encourage the professional training and further training of journalists;
- to encourage relations and mutual aid between its union members;
- to encourage the creation and development of national unions for journalists;
- to collate information on working conditions in the profession;
- to develop the prestige and strengthen the social role of the profession.

On its 30th anniversary in 1982, the IFJ had 25 affiliated organisations: 19 European, two African, two American, two Asian as well as two associated organisations: one European and the other Asian.

The International Organisation of Journalists, founded in 1946, has the following main objectives:

- the maintenance of peace and the consolidation of friendship between peoples and of international understanding through free, truthful and fair dissemination of information;
- defence of the freedom of the press and of journalists against the influence of monopolies and financial groups;
- defence of all the rights of journalists, struggle for an improvement in their material conditions, dissemination of all possible information on their living and working conditions;
- defence of the right of peoples to receive free and truthful information.

On its 30th anniversary in 1976, the IOJ had members (organisations, groups, commissions or individual members) in 109 countries: 34 in Africa, 25 in Asia, 25 in Europe, 23 in America and two in Oceania.

The two international organisations have had friendly relations since 1973. In 1975, while recognising their differences on such fundamental questions as the freedom of the press and the role of journalists and their unions, they decided to co-operate on practical matters: the sharing of information on economic and social conditions, the exchange of publications, efforts to establish a "card of safe conduct" for journalists on dangerous missions, the conclusion of agreements between national professional organisations, the organisation of joint seminars on problems of professional interest, etc.

SOME ASPECTS OF COLLECTIVE BARGAINING

One of the principal aims of a trade union, if not the most important, is to negotiate working conditions for the staff it represents so that, alongside legislation and regulations, collective agreements can regulate certain aspects, if not all the conditions, of the work of journalists.

Profession: Journalist

Here again, there is a wide range in the scope of application of agreements, the negotiating procedures and the texts of collective agreements.

Scope of application

Two aspects will be considered here: the professional categories involved in the negotiations and the level at which the negotiations are conducted.

As to the groups of staff covered, some agreements embrace several categories in the press undertaking, while others deal with them separately. The Canadian press is an example of the first case. But the collective agreement in that country still contains separate sections on administrative staff, editorial staff, advertising staff and distribution staff; it should be added that, where journalists are concerned, top executives, such as editors, are excluded from the scope of application. Similarly, the national collective agreement in Tunisia regulates not only "journalistic and associated employment" (documentation, photography, editing), but also the "professional technical categories" (composition, page make-up and editing, plate-making and offset laboratory, circulation, binding and packing, service and maintenance).

But most frequently negotiations are conducted separately between the managements of the press groups — or their organisations — and the different sections of the trade unions. In these cases, journalists have the advantage of negotiating on the basis of collective agreements which concern them alone. Thus, the national collective agreement on journalists' working conditions in the French press was signed by ten organisations representing sections of the press and by five journalists' unions. In Italy, the representation of the social partners is simpler inasmuch as the only parties present are, on the employers' side, the Italian Federation of Newspaper Publishers and, on behalf of journalists, the National Federation of the Italian Press. In the same way, there are only two parties present at the negotiating table in the Netherlands: the Association of Newspaper Publishers and the Union of Journalists.

As can be seen from the above examples, negotiations take place either at the national level or at the level of the press groups. In many countries, such as, for example, France, the national agreement, which is valid for the whole country, acts as a basis for agreements made at company level, in the sense that the measures in the national agreement replace those of any other agreement which could be less advantageous to journalists; thus, agreements at company level can only improve the conditions stipulated in the national agreement: this happens in particular where long service bonuses, leave, social security, etc., are concerned. In the Netherlands, there are several agreements at the national

Industrial relations

level, relating to different types of press publications (dailies, etc.), while at the company level negotiations deal with such matters as the organisation of work within the editorial department, but not with salaries. In Sweden, a national agreement has been concluded between the Swedish Newspaper Publishers' Association and the Swedish Journalists' Union, this agreement itself having been influenced by the results of the central negotiations between the Confederation of Swedish Employers and the Swedish Confederation of Unions, even though the Newspaper Publishers' Association is not affiliated to the former; this agreement serves as a reference point for negotiations on salaries which are held at the level of individual press establishments.

In the United Kingdom, the Newspaper Publishers Association has not succeeded in having collective bargaining held only at the national level.[6] The chequered history of industrial relations within the British press in the seventies was no incentive to the chapels of the National Union of Journalists to give up their right to negotiate agreements with companies. So the two levels of negotiation still exist, with company agreements stipulating that none of the clauses in them can establish conditions inferior to those in the national agreement. Where there are several chapels for journalists in the same press group, they co-operate and have a mutual exchange of information, but they can, on occasions, negotiate separately. Conversely, when a chapel has members employed with two newspapers, it negotiates agreements with both of them.

Procedures

The preceding paragraphs give some indication of negotiating procedures and in particular of the relation between national and local negotiations where agreements are concluded on both levels. It simply remains to add a few words on certain aspects of negotiating procedures in various countries.

Like most salaried staff in Australia, journalists are in the main protected by "arbitration awards" or by "registered" collective agreements. Under the arbitration and conciliation system which is a characteristic of this country, union organisations draw up a list of claims which can become the object of negotiations between the parties outside or within the arbitration system. Disagreements are submitted to an independent Conciliation and Arbitration Commission which makes a judgement if the parties fail to reach agreement. Awards made by the Commission have the force of law. Similarly, industrial agreements are registered by the Conciliation and Arbitration Commission and are considered to all intents and purposes as awards.

In the largest press group in Sierra Leone, all negotiations between employer and employee take place within a staff committee consisting of a member of each department and the managing director, assisted by those management executives whose presence is deemed by the managing director to be necessary for a particular meeting; this committee meets once a month. The same kind of procedure applies to the joint committee provided for by the 1946 law on professional journalists in Argentina; these committees have the authority to deal with those matters relating to pay, hours and conditions of work which are not regulated by the 1946 law. In Japan, also, there are negotiating committees or joint councils.

The Federal Republic of Germany is a special case inasmuch as it has two kinds of collective agreements: those negotiated by the unions and those negotiated by company committees. The latter may only deal with questions which have not been the subject of agreements at local, regional or national level and the union has the power to negotiate at a higher level than that of the establishment.

How often negotiations take place is extremely variable. Sometimes the times are laid down in the agreements. For example, the collective agreements for the French and Italian press are signed for two years; they are thereafter renewable from year to year by tacit consent, unless otherwise requested by one of the parties in advance of the renewal date (five months' notice in Italy and six in France). In one of the Malaysian newspaper groups, negotiations are held every three years. In the Canadian press, the validity of collective agreements varies from 12 to 18 months, with the option to renew with or without amendments. In many countries, no particular period is laid down since negotiations can take place whenever requested by one of the parties.

Content

As has been noted in the two preceding sections on the scope of application of collective agreements and on negotiating procedures, in some countries different subjects are shared between different levels of negotiation. Examples of such subject division are to be found in the Federal Republic of Germany and the Netherlands (where it is perhaps more marked). But in most countries where conditions of employment and work are regulated by collective agreements, in the absence of, or as a complement to, legislative measures, these agreements cover a vast range of subjects. Numerous examples have already been given and these need not be repeated. It is sufficient to mention two particularly notable statements on the range of subjects covered by agreements. The first is to be found in the first article of the agreement concluded between the Irish Press and the National Union of Journalists in Ireland: "Every journalist is required to read this booklet carefully as it contains his terms of employment, job definitions and procedural and disciplinary machinery". The second is extracted from the first article of the Collective

Bargaining Program of the Newspaper Guild in the United States which is periodically updated: "A contract between the Guild and employer is a listing of the rights and privileges guaranteed to the employees by the employer".

Freelance journalists and collective bargaining

At several points in this study, there have been references to the precarious situation of freelance journalists, on account of their status. This can be attributed, among other causes, to the fact that they are not regarded as employees and are thus more often than not excluded from the scope of application of collective agreements. However, trade unions in several countries have long been trying either to negotiate special agreements with press undertakings for freelance journalists or to obtain their inclusion in the general agreements by means of special measures. Certain recent legislative measures (see Chapter 1, "Professional status", and corresponding note 10) have the same objective: a law of 1974 in the Federal Republic of Germany allows certain categories of independent workers, including journalists, to conclude collective agreements.

In Denmark, there is an agreement on minimum amounts to be paid for press photographs and documents submitted by independent contributors. In France, although the national collective agreement has nothing to say on the subject of freelance journalists, the prices paid for freelance contributions — texts, photographs, drawings — are included in the rates negotiated at company level. Separate agreements for the benefit of independent contributors have been concluded in several companies in the Netherlands. In the United Kingdom, the National Union of Journalists includes a section for freelance workers and the section is represented in national negotiations on minimum rates to be paid to freelance workers; but there is no link between the increases in these minimum rates and the increases in the minimum rates of staff journalists. In Sweden, there is a special collective agreement for freelancers which covers the same sectors as the collective agreement for journalists, but it is applicable only to those who are members of the union.

The 1982 version of the collective agreement in the French-speaking part of Switzerland is one of the most favourable to freelance journalists. It first of all defines what is meant by this term: "The freelance journalist is any active member of the Swiss Federation of Journalists who is entered on the professional register and who collaborates with a publication which is a member of the Newspaper Union of French-speaking Switzerland in some legally recognised way other than a work contract but who, on the other hand, is not employed full time as a reporter". The agreement goes on to specify some of the journalists' rights, in particular on the subject of pay. This must take into account the difficulty of the assignment, the conditions in which it is performed, the time required (including travelling), the quality of the work supplied and its possible exclusiveness; pay may not be below the minimum fixed in the collective agreement. The methods of paying the journalist may be payment based on time spent on the job, a monthly retainer, payment for the article or photographic story, payment by the line, payment per photo, or payment in a lump sum. All contributions accepted must be paid for within 30 days. Finally, after supplying a fixed number of contributions for two years in an overall period of four years, freelance journalists have the right, as of the third year, to 20 per cent of their average fees during the two preceding years.

However, such a collective agreement, with its emphasis on the interests of freelance journalists, is somewhat rare. Most measures, if they exist, seldom go further than the establishment of minimum rates.

LABOUR DISPUTES

Even though they affect relatively few workers, press disputes invariably arouse widespread attention. When newspapers do not appear in the shops or news programmes on radio or television are reduced, daily life is disrupted — a reminder of the vital role played by the media in modern society. It is difficult for the public to know who to blame for these temporary periods of silence: is it the owners, or the trade unions? And if the latter, who has stopped work: the journalists or other categories of staff, in particular the printers?

Moreover, such disputes are extreme cases; it is rare for a dispute to go as far as a work stoppage. It should be pointed out that in certain countries, such as the United Republic of Cameroon or Liberia, journalists do not have the right to strike and in Sweden or Switzerland they must refrain from doing so during the validity period of their collective agreement. As at all workplaces, there are probably numerous individual or group disputes in news-rooms, of which only a tiny number end up by paralysing the publication, the majority being settled through procedures for resolving differences or through negotiation.

The reasons for these differences are also numerous. Some are common to the world of work in general and concern such matters as the structure and amount of pay, the allocation of working time, career advancement, individual transfers to other working positions, etc. Others are peculiar to journalism — those touching on freedom of expression, on participation of the staff in the newspaper's editorial policy, and especially on the introduction of automation, the increasing trend towards concentration of ownership and the other structural changes which have been occurring in the press over the past few years. These phenomena have led to the prolonged collective disputes which have marked the recent history of the press. Generally speaking, these conflicts have affected the entire staff of the newspaper at its production centre and have been all the more severe because the stakes at issue have been more serious than usual and, in the final analysis, the employment of all or part of the staff has been threatened.

In these particular cases, the limitations of the procedures for settling disputes, if indeed such procedures have been used, have been revealed.

This study does not attempt to describe these procedures in different countries, but it may be useful to mention the most interesting features of some of them and of the way in which they are used.

In Australia, a dispute on working conditions quite often occurs in a particular company rather than in the press as a whole, the reasoning being that if a publisher's activities are held up while competitors' newspapers continue to appear, the dispute will have more impact and thus persuade the publisher to seek an agreement. The arbitration awards and "registered" agreements which were mentioned earlier contain measures which authorise employers involved in disputes, individually or as a group, to seek the help of the Conciliation and Arbitration Commission to resolve the conflict to the satisfaction of both parties. Similarly, there is nothing to prevent them from reaching an understanding with the workers' organisations outside the jurisdiction of the Commission.

There are no collective disputes in the United Republic of Cameroon. In the event of individual disputes, when the matter has not been settled by the intervention of the union, an attempt at conciliation is made in the presence of the local inspector for labour and the provident fund, or through the competent jurisdiction for common law: the lower or upper tribunal, according to the importance of the amount in dispute.

The procedure for the solution of disputes in the Canadian press is set out in detail in the collective agreement. Broadly speaking, these agreements point out that it is in the interests of both parties to settle their differences quickly and, if possible, between the journalist as plaintiff, accompanied by the union delegate or not, or even simply represented by the union delegate, and his or her superior. In the absence of a solution within reasonable time, at the same or at a higher level in the company, the parties lay the case before a joint committee composed of employers' and union representatives in equal numbers (normally two persons from each side). This committee must submit its opinion within a fixed time. Failing this, the matter is transferred to an arbitration council whose decision is binding. Under the agreements, the council consists either of three members, two of them representing the parties and the third jointly nominated by them, or of a single arbitrator jointly named by the parties. If they fail to agree on the nomination, the Minister of Labour in the province concerned selects an arbitrator. The arbitration findings must also be rendered within a fixed period. In certain companies, there is no provision for the phase of a joint committee; in that case, the dispute goes directly to arbitration.

A similar procedure is allowed for in the collective agreements signed in the United States and this is not surprising when it is recalled that the agreements are signed by the Newspaper Guild on behalf of editorial staff, as is the case in Canada. However, in the United States, arbitration procedures are based on the rules laid down by the American Association for Arbitration.

In France, the national collective agreement recommends that individual disputes be submitted to a joint committee of conciliation which has conciliation as its sole purpose and which is composed of two employers' representatives and two journalists' representatives. Where required, such a committee can be set up in each region. If one of the parties objects and the attempt at conciliation fails, the interested parties may bring the dispute either before an arbitration commission which makes provision in particular cases for the application of those parts of the Labour Code concerning journalists (dismissal after 15 years of service, application of the conscience clause, charge of serious misdemeanour), or before any other jurisdiction competent to deal with the matter, in particular, the trade court. Similarly, collective disputes are submitted to a regional committee of conciliation consisting of four representatives of the appropriate employers' organisations and four of the journalists' organisations. In the event of failure at this level, they go before a national committee of conciliation, also formed jointly and with the same number of representatives. If disagreement still persists, the dispute is submitted to arbitration, if both parties consent.

It should be added that since 1982 journalists in the public service audio-visual media in France have also come under the national collective agreement and, as a result, must submit any collective disputes to a conciliation committee, in the same fashion as their colleagues in the printed press; but they are obliged to operate a minimum news service on these occasions and this, to some extent, tempers the effect of the strike weapon if the conciliation effort breaks down.

In the Federal Republic of Germany, when differences arise on conditions of work, each of the parties can appeal to a special arbitration council composed of an equal number of representatives of the works council and management. In certain cases, the labour tribunal can initiate the arbitration procedure against the will of one of the parties. When national negotiations on salaries are at a stalemate, normal procedure requires that three negotiators from each side agree on the choice of a conciliator. The latter makes recommendations. If they are not accepted, a commission consisting of five members of each party, chaired by the conciliator who has the right to vote, presents its proposals. Each party has one week to accept or reject them. In the event of rejection by one or the other, a further delay of 48 hours must be observed before a strike can be launched.

In Iraq, in accordance with a recent law on staff journalists, professional differences are settled by inspection committees, reconstituted each year to ensure that the law is applied; they include representatives of the journalists' union, on the one hand, and representatives from the Ministries of Labour, Information and Social Affairs, on the other. The union may also act to settle the differences through conciliation. Recourse to tribunals is possible as well.

In Ireland, disputes arising from the application or interpretation of the collective agreement which cannot be settled with the relevant executive are submitted to an internal committee, as provided for in the agreement. This committee includes four representatives from each party. If it fails to reach an agreement, the matter goes for arbitration to a third party acceptable to both sides. The parties bind themselves not to engage in any direct action until the possibilities of a peaceful settlement have been exhausted.

In Italy, collective or individual differences arising from the national collective agreement are submitted for conciliation to a body set up in each locality in which the regional press association (the union side) has its headquarters. This body consists of two representatives of the regional press association, two from the Federation of Publishers and a fifth member named jointly by the parties. If the attempt at conciliation does not succeed within a month, the parties may resort to the judicial authority.

In Japan, any dispute which the management and staff cannot resolve may be placed before the prefectorial committees or central labour relations boards which have powers of conciliation, mediation or arbitration; they are also competent to pronounce judgements and to order that corrective measures be taken in the event of inequitable working practices. Where individual disputes are concerned, certain companies have set up mechanisms and procedures to study claims; others seek a solution with the help of the union and the personnel department.

In New Zealand, the settling of disputes in the private sector is regulated by the Industrial Relations Act of 1973. This Act draws a distinction between "disputes of interest", i.e., those associated with the negotiation of an award or a collective agreement, and "disputes of rights", i.e., those touching on the interpretation of an award or a collective agreement, including a personal grievance.

Disputes of interest, usually the result of a rejection by the employer of a union claim, are settled: *(a)* by voluntary negotiation, through a joint negotiating committee — the resulting agreement is registered as a collective agreement and binds only the parties involved in the negotiations; *(b)* by conciliation, through a conciliation committee consisting of a fixed number of assessors under the chairmanship of an Industrial Conciliator (without any power of decision) — the agreement which emerges is registered by the Arbitration Court (see below) and binds not only the parties directly concerned but also all persons who subsequently work in the industrial sector in question; *(c)* by arbitration, through the Arbitration Court which, failing a settlement through conciliation, makes an award which has the same coverage as a conciliated collective agreement.

A similar procedure for collective bargaining is followed in Australia. Legal disputes are submitted to a joint committee under the chairmanship of an independent person, usually an industrial conciliator. If the parties fail to reach agreement, the chairman can either make a ruling or refer the dispute to the Arbitration Court. Individual claims are first handled by the immediate superior and, failing an agreement at this level, between the union representative and management. In the event of disagreement at this level, the matter is submitted in writing to a claims committee, with or without a chairman, depending on the decision of the parties involved. The decision of this committee is binding, but if no decision is taken, the case is submitted to an arbitration tribunal for final settlement.

The conditions of work for journalists in the public sector are laid down, under the terms of the State Services Conditions of Employment Act of 1977, by the State Services Commission, which makes its decision after negotiations with the Public Service Association. If these negotiations fail, the matter is taken before a Public Sector Tribunal under the chairmanship of a judge of the Arbitration Court. In the case of legal disputes, normal methods of negotiation between worker and manager are used, and the union can be called on at any stage of the negotiations.

In the United Kingdom, press groups have, in general, concluded agreements for settling disputes with the chapels of the National Union of Journalists or the Institute of Journalists. Procedures are usually at several levels, similar to those in other countries. First the president ("father" or "mother") of the chapel and the relevant editor attempt to reach settlement and subsequently discussions are held between a union or chapel representative and a member of the company's management. In the event of failure at this level, the matter is taken to national level, for example to the Institute of Journalists and the Newspaper Society who, if there is no agreement, can transfer it to a committee of "three plus three" and then a committee of "five plus five", both parties refraining from any hostile action while the procedure is under way. A parallel mechanism is available for the settlement of disputes involving staff other than journalists. The 1976 report of the Advisory Conciliation and Arbitration Service noted that since 1974 journalists' chapels had been more inclined than others to use the "national" procedure. It added that most of the disputes dealt with in this way had been individual conflicts and that, of the collective conflicts, only a small number had concerned the annual company agreements.[7]

In Senegal, the national collective agreement has set up a joint interpretation and conciliation committee, the purpose of which is to achieve an amicable settlement of differences arising from different interpretations of the agreement, or to examine the legality of serious penalties imposed on journalists. If this committee renders a unanimous opinion, it has the same legal weight as the clauses in the agreement. In the event of disagreement, the parties may have recourse to the Labour Inspection Unit.

The collective agreement in the French-speaking part of Switzerland also provides for a joint committee responsible for its application. The committee is made up of seven representatives of the Swiss Federation of Journalists and an equal number from the Newspaper Union of French-speaking Switzerland. Each year it delegates a chairman and a secretary each chosen alternatively from the delegates of the Swiss Federation of Journalists and the Newspaper Union. It is informed of all breaches of the agreement. Its first action is to seek to conciliate the parties. Failing this, it submits a reasonable proposition to them. If one party rejects the proposition of the joint committee, the latter can refer it to the arbitration tribunal which renders a final verdict. This tribunal is composed of two arbitrators, one appointed by the plaintiff, the other by the defendant, and a "supervisory arbitrator" selected by the other two, normally an acting or retired magistrate. The tribunal makes its awards by majority vote. Its primary function is to restore all rights to the injured party. Subsequently, it determines the gravity of the error committed by the other party and issues a warning, allocates blame or imposes a nominal fine; the Union and the Federation are also obliged to make a permanent deposit as a guarantee, each providing half of the maximum amount of the nominal fine. The cantonal or regional sections of the Union and the Federation can set up a smaller joint committee at their level, endowed with the same conciliation functions and with other functions as well; in the event of failure, the dossier is transmitted to the national joint committee which handles it as described above.

PARTICIPATION OF JOURNALISTS IN DECISION-MAKING

Collective bargaining on employment and working conditions and the joint mechanisms for settling disputes represents one of the most firmly established forms of co-operation between press employers and workers, at least in a large number of countries. But in this sector, as in others, there have been innovations in industrial relations which give the unions the right to information, if not consultation, on the main problems affecting the progress of the company; the boldest of these new trends even gives unions the right to participate in decision-making.

The main issues on which unions claim the right to be informed are for the most part fairly limited.

First of all there is the matter of the newspaper's editorial policy. What is meant by this is not so much the basic choice — it is conceded by a large majority that this choice must be made by the owner or publisher — as the attitude of the newspaper towards new questions or events on which the basic editorial policy does not dictate a precise line of action.

Next come certain aspects of the management of editorial staff: recruitment, dismissal, choice of editorial heads.

Then there are decisions on the adoption of new composition and printing techniques which are designed to increase the profitability of the publication, but which could affect both job security for all types of staff and could, to some extent, affect the nature of the journalist's work.

Finally, there are structural problems which might lead to the decline of the newspaper and, as a result, a change in its fundamental policy — against which the conscience clause, if it is valid, offers only precarious protection — or to its disappearance.

The authors of the Declaration of Munich [8] must have been aware of the huge obstacles in the way of achieving their objectives, if the modesty of their claims is any guide: "The editorial staff has obligatorily to be informed on all important decisions which may influence the life of the enterprise. It should be at least consulted before a definitive decision on all matters related to the composition of the editorial staff, e.g. recruitment, dismissals, mutations and promotion of journalists, is taken".

Information on some subjects, consultation on others — this was only a minimum platform and the authors were still far from setting as their objective the institution of industrial democracy in the press. The International Federation of Journalists went much further in its Declaration of 1972 on the internal freedom of the press. While recognising that it was up to the owner or publisher to define the basic political line of the newspaper, the IFJ laid down the principle that any change in this policy should be agreed on between the owner or publisher and the journalists. The editorial team could not be changed without the consent of the editor and the head of the department concerned. Nominations to key posts in the editorial section could not take effect if three-quarters of the staff journalists with at least one year of service were against them. The interests of journalists had to be represented at employer level by elected committees or delegates. Staff journalists had to be informed and consulted before any decisions relating to the editorial team or any which might have technical, administrative, economic or financial consequences on the editorial staff were taken. At its Congress in Lugano in 1982, the

Industrial relations

IFJ reiterated its claims for editorial freedom. It also developed the idea of the need for a formal structure which would give journalists the right to be consulted on, and to take part in, any decisions relating to editorial policy.

But what is the real state of affairs in different countries?

Three different approaches are evident. In that of the first group of countries — Ghana, Guyana, Honduras, Hong Kong, Ireland, Malaysia, for example — there is no formal procedure for information, consultation or participation in decision-making. In these countries, journalists are seldom involved in decisions or, if they are, their involvement is simply on an individual and informal basis. Australia is a special case in the sense that neither the Federal Parliament, which has only limited powers in the area of industrial relations (according to a reply by the Government), nor the State Parliaments, have introduced any legislation on the participation of employees; in practice, the degree of participation varies from one press group to another, depending on its internal policy and size, and where there is any, it is purely informal. The same seems to apply to New Zealand.

In the second group of countries, there are formal structures for information, consultation and even co-operation, set up through legislation for the benefit of salaried staff, or through collective agreements specially designed for the press. However, even these mechanisms do not open the doors to genuine participation in decision-making, as can be seen from the following examples.

Under the terms of one collective agreement in Canada, there must be a meeting between management and staff at least once every six months, in every department (including the editorial department). Ideas and suggestions on the activities of the department are exchanged. The departmental head must be present and there must not be more than six staff representatives. In the same country, another agreement has established a recruitment committee, consisting of the director, the editor and two journalists, responsible for examining applications from candidates and for giving an opinion; the final power of decision lies in the hands of the director. The internal committee meets five times a year to examine the financial situation. An information committee of three management representatives and four journalists meets once a week and is competent to deal with editorial policy.

The national contract for Italian journalists stipulates that any company engaged in producing a daily newspaper or periodical or any daily news agency, with at least ten reporters, must create an editorial committee. This committee, composed of three members elected by the annual general meeting of reporters, is responsible for protecting the moral and material rights of journalists as set out in the national contract and by legislation. Its special function is to ensure that the contract is applied to the letter, to take action to ensure adherence to social legislation and to act as a conciliator in the event of individual or collective disputes. In addition, it gives advice and formulates proposals on technical and professional questions, the organisation of the newsroom, working hours, staff changes and dismissals; in particular, this committee must be asked for its views on any changes which may lead to the resignation of a journalist. It also provides its views and submits proposals on any activity which may affect the structure of the company and thereby jeopardise the specific rights of journalists. To exercise these functions, the committee must receive the necessary information from the employer. If the company employs fewer than ten reporters, the staff elect a delegate who enjoys the same powers. Editorial departments detached from the parent company, if they have at least ten members with the right to vote, also elect a delegate who forms part of the central editorial committee. In the case of companies producing several publications, the editorial committee is elected by the entire journalistic staff. Moreover, a delegate is elected to this committee for each publication which employs at least ten reporters if it is not already represented on the editorial committee.

In Japan, most press establishments have set up joint consultative committees through which management explains to union representatives the policy and plans of the enterprise. Here again it is usually a question of a unilateral exercise. However, in the collective agreement for one of the television companies, it is stipulated that management must consult the union and take its opinion into consideration on the following subjects: establishment of the budget, organisation of work, professional grading, rules on the allocation of work, questions connected with the basic policy of the company, etc. But, as will be seen later, only one large newspaper has set up a real system of participation in decision-making.

In Pakistan, the right to participate in decision-making has been established by labour laws for all workers and, consequently, for journalists as well. To this end, there are joint management councils which are concerned with improvements in working conditions and with industrial relations. But outside these sectors, the Government's view is that the union submits opinions rather than participates in decision-making.

In the Netherlands, the Association of Newspaper Publishers and the Union of Journalists have reached an agreement by which, as of 1977, each press enterprise adopts a joint "editorial statute" which gives journalists the right to be consulted on the nomination of the editor and allows them to present their own list of candidates; it also gives them the right to be consulted on all matters relating to the organisation of work within the editorial department. Thus, editorial committees have been created in many companies.[9]

In the United Kingdom, a large number of collective agreements contain a clause on the obligation of management to consult with the union regularly on subjects of common interest. Some of them specifically exclude editorial policy from these "subjects of common interest", and nowhere does this appear as a matter of consultation between the two parties. Management problems also remain a closed preserve for managements. However, there is one case of an agreement by which management commits itself to supply the maximum possible information on the company to the union and to open its books to an accountant chosen by mutual agreement; the union feels that the report by such an expert helped in obtaining a considerable increase in salaries.[10] But in fact the most common situation is that in which management and the union declare the need for co-operation and agree to consult with each other on all important matters affecting the work and conditions of journalists, before taking final decisions; in addition, the father or mother of the chapel must be given advance notice on any recruitment or dismissal of a journalist. The Royal Commission on the Press recommended in 1977 that journalists should be involved in the nomination of their editors. In its view, editors appointed in this way would gain the support of the editorial team more easily. However, the Commission laid down no precise conditions to this end, in view of the wide diversity of the press.[11]

In Switzerland, by virtue of the agreement concluded between the Swiss Association of Newspaper Publishers and the Swiss Federation of Journalists, the publisher is obliged to consult journalists on all important decisions concerning the newspaper, in so far as these decisions could affect their personal or professional situation. This concerns, in particular, decisions of a professional, technical, administrative or financial nature and those concerned with the composition of the editorial team: recruitment, dismissals and transfers.

Another example of co-operation comes from Tunisia where the national collective agreement for press enterprises has created joint consulting committees. Such a committee must operate in any establishment where at least 20 people are normally employed. It is composed of three titular members, including the chairman, and three deputy members, representing the employer, and three titular and three deputy members elected by the staff in each of the administration, technical and editorial departments. The committee watches over the application of the collective agreement. It makes suggestions on all matters affecting the staff, studies the general rules on promotion and co-operates in the establishment of a promotion system. It also expresses its opinion on transfers and on changes of work allocation, examines matters relating to training and refresher courses, participates in the creation and application of measures concerning retirement and social benefits and, finally, acts as a disciplinary council. In short, its competence is primarily in the field of staff management, where it plays an essentially consultative but important role, whereas the political and economic management of the publication is totally out of its hands. It should also be noted that of the three titular members who represent the staff, only one is a journalist.

Where the press is concerned, therefore, these countries are a long way from the practices which are the hallmark of an "industrial democracy". But newspapers in a third group of countries come much closer to this concept.

In the Federal Republic of Germany, the 1972 Works Constitution Act stipulates that, in any establishment with a permanent staff of at least five employees aged 18 or more, a works council must be elected for co-operation and co-determination purposes, its size being increased with the growth of the company.[12] The general powers of the council are to watch over the application of the laws and regulations in force under collective agreements, to propose measures to the employer in the interests of the establishment and of the staff and to deal with workers' claims; if it finds that the claims are justified, it intercedes with the employer to obtain settlement and, if there is disagreement, it can take the matter up with a conciliation committee. The council is also involved in such matters as company discipline, working hours, leave plans, safety, health, social work, criteria for and levels of pay, performance bonuses, etc. With regard to staff management, it is kept informed on current and future needs and on the relevant professional training programmes. Instructions on the transfer of staff are submitted for approval by the council. It is also consulted on the introduction and organisation of professional training facilities in the establishment, and participates in deciding how they should be implemented. The council shares in management decisions on measures affecting staff. In all establishments which usually employ more than 100 persons, a finance committee is created which is responsible for studying financial questions with the employer and informing the works council thereon. Under the heading "financial questions" fall such matters as the economic and financial situation of the establishment, production and investment programmes, rationalisation projects, the adoption of new methods of work, mergers, etc. In addition, in establishments with more than 20 regular employees with the right to vote, the employer is obliged to supply the works council with detailed information on changes in the establishment which could have negative effects on the staff and to examine these changes jointly with the council.

As can be seen, these different areas of information, consultation or co-management are of the greatest interest to journalists who, like workers in any other establishment, are normally entitled to vote and to be elected. More particularly, the works councils' rights with respect to staff management and financial information are of utmost importance to journalists at a time when the press is undergoing major structural and technological changes. However, the law contains various limitations, of which two could affect journalists. The first concerns all establishments and affects employees holding certain management posts to which the

Industrial relations

law is not applicable (paragraph 5.3), although the persons concerned can be nominated as members of the finance committee (paragraph 107.1) or attend its meetings in the capacity of specialists alongside the employer (paragraph 108.2). The second concerns establishments involved in political, artistic or educational activities, in particular those whose purpose is to provide information or comment (paragraph 118): such establishments are not subject to the 1972 law when the particular character of the establishment is opposed to it. In the view of the Government, there could be numerous occasions when this clause would be applicable to journalists, and the Federal Labour Tribunal has on several occasions had to intervene to specify the rights of the works council in this area.

It should be added that the federal or regional laws dealing with staff representatives are applicable to journalists employed in the public sector, and especially to those employed in the radio and television networks.

In France,[13] the law provides for the staff to be represented within all establishments, including press ones, employing at least ten salaried persons. The representatives are either elected by the staff or appointed through agreement with the trade union bodies. Their main task is to submit to the employers individual or collective claims which have not been settled directly. In the absence of a workers' committee, they assume some of the consultative and advisory functions normally performed by such a body.

Most establishments with at least 50 employees have workers' committees and journalists participate in them in the same way as other workers. These committees consist of the head of the establishment, or a representative, and a delegation from the staff, the number of members depending on the number of salaried employees. The committees are consulted on matters relating to conditions of employment, staff and professional training. They supervise or control the management of the social programmes established for the benefit of the salaried staff. They study measures conceived by management or suggested by the staff to improve the productivity of the establishment. They have the right to be informed and consulted on questions relating to the organisation, management and general development of the establishment, and particularly on problems of staffing and working hours; they are consulted at all times on staff reductions and their views on intended measures are transmitted to the labour inspection unit. A report is given to them at least once a year on the activity of the establishment, its turnover, the salary structure and increases in salary levels. When the establishment becomes a limited liability company, the management is also obliged to make available to the committee the profit and loss account, the annual balance sheet, the accountants' report and all other documents which it plans to submit to the general meeting of shareholders. In the case of companies, a delegation of the committee attends the meetings of the board of directors in a consultative capacity.

But here again, it is a question of information and consultation rather than real participation in decision-making. A certain number of newspapers have taken another step towards co-management on a more or less long-term basis. The phenomenon began during the fifties and developed in the sixties in the form of "editorial committees".[14] The first one was set up at *Le Monde*; numerous companies have followed this example but, for the most part, the committees have subsequently disappeared; however, the committee at *Le Monde* is still in existence, with certain modifications. It is perhaps interesting to describe briefly the more unusual aspects of the management system set up within this newspaper, first, because of its uniqueness, and second, because it has served as a reference point for other experiments and studies in Europe and overseas: for example, a firm of consultants in the United Kingdom, which was commissioned by the National Union of Journalists to study the possibility of converting the Times Publishing Company into one or several workers' co-operatives, made frequent mention of the example at *Le Monde*.[15]

At the present time, the SARL (*Société à responsabilité limitée*: Limited liability company) of *Le Monde* consists of three types of associates who share the capital. Associates A are actual persons, 14 in number, who hold 40 per cent of the partnership shares. Associates B are staff companies, that is the editorial company (40 per cent), the executive company (5 per cent) and the employees' company (4 per cent). Associates C are the acting managers (11 per cent). It is considered at the newspaper that the predominant shareholding of the staff companies, and the impossibility of transferring shares without the agreement of the other associates, prevents any other economic or political group from taking over *Le Monde*.[16] In passing, it is worth noting the weight of the editorial company in this structure. This company alone possesses a minority power to block "extraordinary" decisions, those relating to modifications of the statutes, which require a majority equal to three-quarters of the capital stock; it also plays an important role in other so-called "ordinary" decisions for which a majority of 50 per cent is required. The SARL is administered by one or several managers, including the managing director of the publication, elected by the general assembly which decides on a majority vote of associates representing at least three-quarters of the capital stock (Article 16 of the statutes). Here again, the great influence of the editorial company can be observed. There is also a supervisory council consisting by law of former managers of the council, the legal representatives of the staff companies and a representative of the bearers of A shares. This council has the chairman of the editorial company as its legal chairman. It expresses its views to the managers on the financial policy of the SARL — but can in no case

Industrial relations

interfere in the direction or management of the company — and submits a report on the development of the company to the ordinary general meeting each year.

The editorial company is composed exclusively of card-carrying journalists who work as reporters on *Le Monde* for a monthly salary.

To give a full idea of the power of the journalists on this publication, it should be added that they can also express their views through two other bodies: the editorial committee, which determines the editorial policy, and the committee on salaries, which decides on general or individual pay increases.

A Japanese newspaper, the *Sankei Shimbun*, represents another example of participation in decision-making. It stands out in this respect from other Japanese newspapers which, as has been seen, adopt a somewhat reserved attitude on this question. This example obviously carries the stamp of "Japanese-style" industrial relations which are characterised by the sense of identification with the company, a characteristic common to most employees in this country. A collective agreement concluded in 1974 provides that the chairman of the union participates as an observer in monthly meetings of the board of directors, and as a full member in weekly meetings of department heads. In addition, a joint council, in which the vice-president of the company and the main departmental heads participate, on the one side, and the trade union secretariat, on the other, holds meetings once a month. A financial crisis in 1976 led both parties to conclude an agreement on a three-year plan of reorganisation aimed at developing closer co-operation between them and initiating a programme of economy which involved salary adjustments and staff reductions (obtained through transfers and non-renewal of fixed term contracts). The chairman of the union was nominated as auditor of the company's accounts and certain of his colleagues were named members of the "reorganisation committee" which was set up to deal with the situation.

But it is probably in Scandinavia that, in journalism as in other sectors of activity, the most developed forms of industrial democracy are to be found.

In Norway, for example, a collective agreement signed in 1973 allows press staff a third of the seats on their company's board of directors if the company employs more than 15 persons (whereas the law on participation in the management of limited liability companies grants this right to the staff only if the permanent staff exceeds 50 employees).[17] Each of the three sections of a newspaper — editorial, technical, administrative — appoints its representative. If there are only two seats available, a rotating system enables the three sections to take turns in being represented. The elected members are entitled to speak and vote on the management of the enterprise and have full rights of inspection on the economic situation of the newspaper, the planning of its activities, etc.

They have the same rights and obligations as the members of the board elected by the shareholders, except that they are excluded from voting on matters relating to the fundamental policy of the newspaper and from appointing the editor or the holder of any important post which has a direct connection with this policy. However, they have the right to express their views on these questions. Moreover, the management must supply the staff delegates with full information on any changes contemplated in the activities of the company, its economic situation, any expansion projects or any other projects directly affecting the editorial department, including staff changes. In many newspapers, the editorial staff has won the right to make its own staff appointments.

In Sweden, the 1972 law on the Representation of Employees on the Boards of Joint-stock Companies and Profit-making Associations [18] grants the staff of these companies or associations, provided that at least 100 workers are employed (a figure subsequently reduced to 25), the right to nominate two members, and a deputy for each of them, to the board of directors. In addition, the law of 1976 on Co-determination at Work [19] obliges establishments to conclude collective agreements to define the rights of workers in this field. The union enjoys a "priority" right of interpretation in the event of differences on the application of these agreements and can veto agreements on subcontracting or similar arrangements which appear to be contrary to the law, the collective agreement or the accepted practice in the branch of activity or the profession. However, certain exceptions limit the scope of this second law: for example, establishments "whose objective is to influence public opinion" are exempt from its application, in so far as the objectives of their activities are at issue (Article 2); as a result, journalists do not have the right to influence the political tendencies of their newspaper. In addition, the collective agreement between the Newspaper Publishers' Association and the Swedish Journalists' Union contains a joint declaration by the two partners which specifies certain aspects of co-management. The final result of these various texts is that the management must consult editorial staff on the choice of both departmental heads and other members of the editorial team, as well as on the definition of general policy. Moreover, the principle of joint decision-making is applicable to the establishment of the editorial budget, to decisions on the possible cessation of the publication or of the radio or television programme, and to decisions on an eventual merger or restructuring if they involve a modification of the character or policy of the publication or programme.[20]

* * *

In conclusion, it may be said that for the journalist, as for other workers, the democratisation of life at work is a continuous process; progress is slow and real breakthroughs are rare. In the broad sense of the term, democratisation has been accepted, as is exemplified by the

Industrial relations

freedom of journalists in most countries to form and join unions of their choice — even if, in practice, the numerous evasive tactics adopted to frustrate the exercise of this right, overt or covert, are to be deplored. The proof lies in the wide network of national or local collective agreements by which journalists can have a voice in their conditions of employment and work, and the wide variety of mechanisms through which differences in press enterprises can be settled. However, if "democratisation of work" is to be given its more precise meaning of participation in decisions on the development of the newspaper, whether it is a question of financial results, personnel policy, structure, orientation, or even survival, far less has been achieved: on this level, journalists are often informed but less often consulted, and only in a few enterprises are they normally in a position to count where fundamental decisions are at stake.

Notes

[1] ILO: *Conditions of work and life of journalists*, op. cit., pp. 30 ff.

[2] *Legislative Series* (Geneva, ILO), 1976 — UK 1. This law modifies the Trade Union and Labour Relations Act, 1974 (1974 — UK 1), which itself repealed the Industrial Relations Act, 1971 (1971 — UK 1). These last two laws consecrate the practice of the "closed shop".

[3] Royal Commission on the Press: *Final report*, op. cit., p. 163.

[4] On the organisation of British trade unions — for journalists and printers — in chapels within each newspaper, see K. Sisson: *Industrial relations in Fleet Street* (Oxford, Basil Blackwell, 1975), pp. 97 ff.; and ACAS, op. cit., pp. 80 ff.

[5] G. Fodor and T. Szecskö: *Communication policies in Hungary* (Paris, UNESCO Press, 1974), p. 49.

[6] ACAS, op. cit., pp. 164 ff.

[7] ibid., p. 167.

[8] Declaration adopted in November 1971 by the journalists' unions in the six countries of the European Community (see Chapter 4).

[9] ACAS, op. cit., p. 224.

[10] ibid., p. 170.

[11] Royal Commission on the Press: *Final report*, op. cit., p. 156.

[12] *Legislative Series* (Geneva, ILO), 1972 — Ger.F.R. 1.

[13] See Labour Code, Articles 420 and 431-438 (*Legislative Series* (Geneva, ILO), 1981 — Fr. 1).

[14] Auby and Ducos-Ader, op. cit., pp. 203-210.

[15] *Co-operative possibilities for Times Newspaper Limited*, Study prepared by Jo Ownership Ltd. for the Times' chapel of the National Union of Journalists (February 1979).

[16] See "Les structures de la SARL 'Le Monde'", in *Le Monde* (Paris), 6 July 1982, p. 38.

[17] *IFJ Information* (Brussels, International Federation of Journalists), Vol. XXXI, 1981, pp. 21-22.

[18] *Legislative Series* (Geneva, ILO), 1972 — Swe. 1.

[19] ibid., 1976 — Swe. 1. See also A. Bouvin: "New Swedish legislation on democracy at the workplace", in *International Labour Review* (Geneva, ILO), Mar.-Apr. 1977, p. 131.

[20] See, on the overall question of participation in decision-making, W. Klinkenberg: "Rights and internal democracy of editorial staff in press, radio and television", in *IFJ Information*, op. cit., pp. 5-9.

CONCLUSION

Compared with journalists of the past as portrayed in the first ILO study of over half a century ago, today's journalists are in many ways a privileged group. What will life be like for the journalists of tomorrow?

The improvement in the social condition of journalists can be attributed to the fact that, like other workers, they have benefited from the economic and social development of recent years. But they themselves have been an active element in this general development. They have acted as communications agents, and communications have encouraged progress in all fields. In addition, they have succeeded in achieving better conditions in their own profession, principally through collective bargaining.

Moreover, there is reason to believe that various recent examples of international co-operation have tended to bring about improvements in the profession of journalism. In this context, three documents referred to in Chapter 8 should again be mentioned: the additional Protocol to the Geneva Conventions, the Final Act of the Helsinki Conference on Security and Co-operation in Europe, and the UNESCO Declaration on the Fundamental Principles concerning the Contribution of the Mass Media to Strengthening Peace and International Understanding, to the Promotion of Human Rights, and to Countering Racialism, Apartheid and Incitement to War. These three documents have a particular significance for the security of those working in the information field, both in their own countries and overseas. Of wider interest and more directly related to this study is the *Compendium of principles and good practices relating to the conditions of work and employment of professional workers* which was drawn up at a tripartite meeting of the ILO in 1977 and which is applicable to, among others, "those who are employed in the media". This document deals with the following subjects: freedom of association and collective bargaining, job security, education and training, working conditions and environment and participation in decision-making.[1]

Profession: Journalist

Whatever the real impact of these documents, which moreover can be measured only in the long term and to the extent that governments and professional organisations put them to good use, journalists of today are generally better off than their predecessors.

They are better equipped on the technical level, not only because they have more in-service opportunities to train and develop their professional skills, but also because of the availability of working tools which editors and reporters of 50, or even 20, years ago could only dream about.

They are also better protected than before against the risk of unemployment.

Although they usually still work irregular hours, they have obtained considerably more leave and leisure time; there is continuous progress in this area.

Generally speaking, they are better guaranteed against the risk of sickness, accident, invalidity, death, etc.

They can bargain collectively, no longer just as individuals, on working conditions and can even participate in decisions on the running of their newspaper in certain cases.

However, there is a reverse side to the coin — a side which concerns journalists of today and which will perhaps concern their successors even more. To borrow McLuhan's term, a profound change is shaking up the "Gutenberg galaxy". For some time journalists have been worried by the threat of electronic editing, but they have learned to live with it: they have concluded agreements which, in return for certain concessions on their part, have provided them with solid guarantees, at least for the period of transition. The typographers have been the main losers in the great technological changes in the press.

But this transformation is not yet at an end. The printed press still has golden years ahead of it. Radio and television news programmes will probably not do any more harm to the press than they have done so far and, in any case, these programmes cannot be produced without journalists. But there is a new danger on the horizon: it is the television set coupled to the individual computer terminal — or some other apparatus of the future based on a similar principle — connected to an information centre (news agency or data bank). If such systems become the general rule, it can be assumed that radio or television news programmes — combined with brief information items on local and practical matters and constantly updated — which anyone can switch on to the screen at any time, will be enough to satisfy the daily appetite for news. In such circumstances, the need for daily newspapers can only fade, whereas periodicals, which are relied on for reflection rather than information, will have a growing market.

Perhaps all this is fiction or still only distant reality. But electronic editing seemed a technician's fantasy only 20 years ago, and now it is

Conclusion

yearly conquering new territory. Other forms of media are biding their time, awaiting only a relaxation of the legislation which at present stands in their way and a massive injection of capital, including funds currently invested in the printed press.

These new media will certainly need journalists. But how many? And will they need the same type of journalist? For the product launched on the market will consist of concise information, headlines rather than articles, the latter being virtually reserved for periodicals and specialised publications. Thus a large number of journalists will have to adapt themselves in order to find a place among the new information specialists — or go elsewhere.

The arrival of the linotype machine in the last century, far from being a threat to the printed press, gave it a new lease of life. The electronic editing age has transformed the traditional methods of composition and printing and has seriously affected a whole sector of craftsmen, but it has still not compromised the future of the printed press. The general installation of tele-information at home and at work presents more serious risks, at least for daily newspapers.

This development will probably not occur in the immediate future: economic and cultural factors will no doubt hold it up. Moreover, there is no need to play the devil's advocate: as with all technical progress, this development will naturally have its positive aspects. But it would behove those whose responsibility it is to reflect and decide — in the press world, first of all, as well as in political, trade union and social science circles — to devote their thoughts while there is still time to the many different aspects of a problem which certainly concerns journalists but also concerns the whole of our society.

Note

[1] See Appendix for extracts from this code.

APPENDIX

EXTRACTS FROM THE *COMPENDIUM OF PRINCIPLES AND GOOD PRACTICES RELATING TO THE CONDITIONS OF WORK AND EMPLOYMENT OF PROFESSIONAL WORKERS,* ADOPTED BY AN ILO TRIPARTITE MEETING ON CONDITIONS OF WORK AND EMPLOYMENT OF PROFESSIONAL WORKERS (GENEVA, 22-30 NOVEMBER 1977)

General remarks

. . . .

7. Professional workers should enjoy at least the standards of protection laid down for all workers in national legislation.

Freedom of association and collective bargaining

8. Professional workers should have the right freely to establish and to join appropriate organisations of their own choosing.

9. Professional workers should enjoy adequate protection against acts of anti-union discrimination in respect of their employment. Such protection should apply more particularly in respect of acts calculated to:
(a) make their employment subject to the condition that they shall not join a union or shall relinquish trade union membership;
(b) cause their dismissal or otherwise prejudice them by reason of their union membership or because of their participation in union activities.

10. The conditions of work and employment of professional workers should be determined as far as possible by collective agreements concluded between the employers or employers' organisations and the appropriate organisations of professional workers concerned. Measures should be taken, where necessary, to encourage and promote voluntary negotiation of such collective agreements.

. . . .

Profession: Journalist

Public placement services

15. The public authorities should establish effective machinery to assist professional workers to find jobs. Where possible, special arrangements should be made within public employment services to handle the problems of professional workers. In major agglomerations, and where the employment situation of professional workers is sufficiently serious to justify such a step, specialised services should be established to cater for professional workers.

. . . .

17. The public employment service should work in close co-operation with the employers' and workers' organisations concerned and with the university placement services and other similar services.

. . . .

Security of employment

21. Termination of employment of professional workers should not take place except where there is a valid reason for such termination connected with their service, capacity or conduct or based on the operational requirements of the undertaking. Where such dismissals take place the reasons for them should be clearly stated and should conform where appropriate to legal requirements or collective agreements.

22. Employers should endeavour to restrict as far as possible the adverse effects of mergers, concentrations, take-overs or other major changes in the structure, general objectives or working methods of their undertakings on the security of employment of professional workers.

23. Professional workers and the organisations which represent them in the undertaking according to national practice should be consulted on any proposed change in the structure, general objectives or working methods of an undertaking which are liable to have prejudicial effects on the employment of professional workers as well as the resulting measures that affect their employment.

24. Before terminating employment of professional workers for reasons connected with the operational requirements of the undertaking, employers should seek all possible alternative solutions and should endeavour to reassign such workers to other equivalent jobs within the undertaking. Where reassignment entails a downgrading, the worker concerned should receive compensation according to national law, collective agreements or national practice. Where the worker is reassigned to a job within the undertaking requiring new qualifications, he should be given the opportunity to undertake the necessary training and be assured of an equivalent income throughout the period of training.

25. Where termination of employment for reasons connected with the operational requirements of the undertaking is unavoidable, employers should endeavour to help professional workers to find equivalent employment; to this end employers should contact the public employment services, and where possible other prospective employers in an endeavour to ensure that the workers affected find new jobs before the expiry of their periods of notice.

. . . .

27. A professional worker whose employment is to be terminated should be entitled to a reasonable period of notice or compensation in lieu thereof. The period of notice should take into account the time spent in the service of the undertaking. During the period of notice the worker should, as far as practicable,

be entitled to a reasonable amount of time off without loss in pay in order to seek other employment.

28. Professional workers when unavoidably unemployed should receive, in accordance with national legislation, collective agreements and national practice, an adequate income during a period of time sufficient for them to find new employment.

Education and training

29. Co-operation among public authorities, educational and training institutes and employers, and workers and their organisations should be developed to ensure that educational and training systems take fully into account the requirements of working life and that young persons who undertake a course of training have the best possible chances of finding employment corresponding to their qualifications and aspirations.

30. Education and training for professional-level employment should provide a basis for continuous adjustment and development throughout the worker's career. It should seek to provide every individual not only with the specialised technical knowledge necessary for a given job but also with a body of general knowledge sufficiently broad and deep to enable him to understand and to influence, individually or collectively, the working and social environment, to discharge his responsibilities within the undertaking and in society and to adapt to changing situations.

. . . .

Personnel utilisation policies

38. Employers should establish and implement personnel policies designed to make full use of and to develop the qualifications and abilities of professional workers.

39. To this end, they should endeavour to assign professional workers to jobs corresponding to their qualifications and abilities and provide them with the training facilities necessary to maintain, adapt and develop those qualifications and abilities.

40. The assignments and the training requirements of professional workers should be reviewed from time to time in the light of the interests of the undertaking and the workers concerned.

41. Employers and professional workers should be aware of the danger that excessive specialisation or a protracted period of service in the same job may weaken an individual's ability to adapt and to improve his occupational skills. They should also recognise the potential benefits of broadening the horizons, and of diversifying the experience of professional workers.

42. Consequently, professional workers should be informed where possible of employment opportunities existing in other departments or regional divisions of the undertaking, and their applications for such posts should be given special consideration if they meet the necessary qualifying conditions.

43. Professional workers might have at their request opportunities to be given temporary leave from the undertaking, without break of the employment relationship, and of working part time in other fields.

Profession: Journalist

Job classification

44. Wherever possible efforts should be made to establish, through collective agreements as appropriate and according to national practice, a system of job classification of posts designed for professional workers in the context of a general classification scheme within an undertaking. The system of job classification for professional workers should take into account various criteria such as the level of qualifications, training and experience, the types of duties and the level of responsibility.

45. Such job classification should be regularly reviewed to take into account the changes in the qualifications offered or required on the employment market.

Mobility

46. The mobility of professional workers from one undertaking, branch of activity or region to another should be encouraged inasmuch as it enables them to improve their career prospects or their employability.

47. Measures should be taken to secure harmonisation of social security benefits and of the different old-age, invalidity and survivors' pensions schemes applicable to professional workers with a view to ensuring maintenance of the latter's acquired rights when they transfer from one scheme to another.

. . . .

Equal opportunities between men and women

50. Women and men should have the right on the same terms to receive education and training for highly qualified jobs.

51. The public authorities, and in particular the school and vocational guidance services, should systematically inform young people of both sexes so that they choose the types of training most likely to offer good prospects of employment and career development.

52. Women and men should enjoy equality of opportunity and treatment for career advancement.

. . . .

Organisation of work and annual leave

57. Because of the character of his work, it is not always possible to measure the working day or working week of a professional worker or to apply strict rules on the subject. However, those provisions in legislation or collective agreements relating to normal working hours should be applied as far as possible to professional workers. The actual hours of work of professional workers should not exceed the limits beyond which their health or their family or social life is liable to suffer.

. . . .

59. Where the remuneration of professional workers does not make allowance for the overtime they may be required to work, special compensation in the form of time off and/or cash should be given for such overtime.

Appendix

60. Professional workers should always have the opportunity to take the annual leave to which they are entitled.

. . . .

Participation in decision-making

70. Consultation or participation by workers or by organisations representing them in the making of decisions affecting working life in the enterprise is gaining increasing attention. Professional workers should have the same opportunities as other workers to be consulted in these decision-making processes in accordance with national legislation or practice.

OHIO UNIVERSITY LIBRARY
Please return this book as soon as you
have finished with it. In order to avoid a

OHIO UNIVERSITY LIBRARIES
1000557420

PN 4797 .B613 1984x
Bohere, G.
Profession, journalist